A Primer On The Absolute
PRIMACY OF CHRIST

Blessed *esis*

Forward by Msgr. Arthur Burton Calkins

A Primer on the Absolute Primacy of Christ, is a book prepared for publication by the Franciscans of the Immaculate [marymediatrix.com], POB 3003, New Bedford, MA, 02741-3003.

Cum Permissu Superiorum

ISBN: 978-1-60114-040-1

Academy of the Immaculate
New Bedford, MA

Ephesians 1:3-10

Blessed be the God and Father of our Lord Jesus Christ, who has blessed us with every spiritual blessing on high in Christ.

Even as He chose us in Him before the foundation of the world, that we should be holy and without blemish in His sight in love.

He predestined us to be adopted through Jesus Christ as His sons, according to the purpose of His will,

unto the praise of the glory of His grace, with which He has favored us in His beloved Son.

In Him we have redemption through His blood, the remission of sins, according to the riches of His grace.

This grace has abounded beyond measure in us in all wisdom and prudence,

so that He may make known to us the mystery of His will according to His good pleasure. And this His good pleasure He purposed in Him

to be dispensed in the fullness of the times: to re-establish all things in Christ, both those in the heavens and those on the earth.

Index of Abbreviations

Contents

Foreword

It is a joy and a privilege for me to offer a word of introduction to this little book by Fr. Maximilian Mary Dean, FI for a variety of reasons. First of all, I am happy to do so because of my close association with the Franciscan Friars of the Immaculate from the very beginnings of their existence as a new religious community sprung from the Marian charism of Saint Francis of Assisi as lived by Saint Maximilian Maria Kolbe and Saint Pio of Pietrelcina. My relationship with them has been a source of countless blessings for me and has given me an ever greater appreciation of the Franciscan heritage in theology and spirituality which enshrines what Saint Maximilian Kolbe referred to as the "golden thread" of the Immaculate. Further, and as an integral component of that fundamental Franciscan-Marian charism, I am especially pleased to share my conviction about the inestimable value of the contribution of Bl. John Duns Scotus to Catholic theology and spirituality and hence to the useful introduction to this master with which Fr. Maximilian Mary has provided us.

I can trace my own attraction to the Subtle Doctor, as Scotus is known, to three specific stages in the course of my own intellectual and spiritual formation besides the on-going influence of the Franciscan Friars of the Immaculate. The first was my initiation into scotistic studies, even if at a very elementary level, in the mid 1980's through the good offices of Fr. James McCurry, OFM Conv. and my fascination with the last great work of the late Fr. Juniper Carol, OFM, *Why Jesus Christ?*[1] which the author kindly autographed for me "with best Scotistic wishes"! The second was my visit to the tomb of Bl. John Duns Scotus in Cologne after the Mariological Congress at Kevelaer on 21 September 1987 in the company of Fr. McCurry. (One must never discount the efficacy of contact with the relics of holy persons.) I still remember the pithy Latin inscription on the tomb: *Scotia me genuit. Anglia me docuit. Gallia me accepit. Colonia me tenet.* [Scotland gave me birth. England taught me. France received me. Cologne holds me.] The third was my presence in the Vatican Basilica on 20 March 1993 for the confirmation of the *cultus* of John Duns Scotus and the beatification of Dina Bélanger, another one of my heavenly friends in whose life the Marian imprint is also very strong. Because of complex historical vicissitudes, the process of the "equivalent beatification" of Scotus had been arrived at only after the solemn promulgation of the Decree *Qui docti fuerint* in the presence of the Holy Father on 6 July 1991 which authoritatively affirmed that "The reputation for sanctity and heroic virtues of the Servant

---

1 JUNIPER B. CAROL, OFM, *Why Jesus Christ?* Thomistic, Scotistic and Conciliatory Perspectives (Manassas, VA: Trinity Communications, 1986). For an excellent appreciation of this work, cf. PETER DAMIAN FEHLNER, OFM CONV., "Fr. Juniper Carol, OFM: His Mariology and Scholarly Achievement," Marian Studies XLIII (1992) 38-42.

of God John Duns Scotus as well as the cultus offered to him from time immemorial are established with certainty." (Just as in the case of venerating relics, I believe that there are special graces which come through the intercession of Saints and Blesseds when they are being elevated to the honors of the altar.)

What I arrived at by degrees—and I believe by intervention of divine providence—Fr. Maximilian Mary has arranged for us in an orderly fashion. As one meditates on the insights of Scotus—and these can readily serve as the theme of our prayer as well as of our study—one begins to see not only the depths of the Subtle Doctor's thought, but even more, the depths of God's divine plan for creation. For this reason, it is a tragedy that such immense prejudice has been shown to the insights of Scotus in the course of the centuries. One can more readily understand the animus against him by English Protestants because of his identification with the Catholic doctrine on the Eucharist and loyalty to the Successor of St. Peter (which issued in his name, "dunce," becoming a synonym for fool) than the incredible bigotry against him which I have personally met in Catholics who seem otherwise to be well educated. The principal reason for this discrimination among Catholic intellectuals, I fear, should not be attributed to St. Thomas Aquinas, but rather to many of his lesser disciples.[2]

What are Scotus' insights, then? The principal ones have to do precisely with Jesus Christ as the absolute center of the created universe and His Mother as next to him in the hierarchy of created being. They have to do with God's eternal plan before time began and before his taking into account—we are speaking in a human way here—the reality of man's fall from grace. As Fr. Maximilian points out with great skill, this is precisely the vision which St. Paul communicates in his great Christological hymns found in Ephesians 1:3-10 and Colossians 1:12-20. It is a marvelously optimistic view of the immensity of God's goodness and of the role of the created human nature of the Son of God, a vision of creation worthy of being drawn out and substantiated by a spiritual son of the Saint who chanted the Canticle of Brother Sun.

It was in fact the bold philosophical thought of Scotus which overcame the objections to Mary's Immaculate Conception. God, who could foresee the fruits of the redemption wrought by Christ, could communicate them in advance to the New Eve so that she could collaborate in the redemption of the rest of us. This is an amazing insight into the divine purposes which Blessed Pius IX codified,

---

2 STEFANO CECCHIN, OFM, *L'Immacolata Concezione. Breve storia del dogma* (Vatican City: Pontificia Academia Mariana Internationalis "Studi Mariologici #5," 2003) 75-99.

so to speak, in *Ineffabilis Deus*, the Apostolic Constitution proclaiming the Immaculate Conception, by stating that "God, by one and the same decree, had established the origin of Mary and the Incarnation of Divine Wisdom." This, in effect, was a confirmation of the thesis sustained by Scotus and his followers for centuries. The late Pope John Paul II beautifully corroborated this fact in his Marian encyclical *Redemptoris Mater* by stating of Mary that

> In the mystery of Christ she is *present* even "before the creation of the world," as the one whom the Father "has chosen" *as Mother* of his Son in the Incarnation. And, what is more, together with the Father, the Son has chosen her, entrusting her eternally to the Spirit of holiness. In an entirely special and exceptional way Mary is united to Christ, and similarly she *is eternally loved in this "beloved Son,"* this Son who is of one being with the Father, in whom is concentrated all the "glory of grace" [*Redemptoris Mater* #8].

In this vision Jesus and Mary are part of God's eternal plan as the crown of creation even before the prevision of original sin. True, they are not on the same level because Jesus is the God-man whereas Mary is only a human creature, but a creature unlike any other. The attentive reader will note that Fr. Maximilian draws out the unique mediatorial role of Mary—always subordinate to that of Jesus—which, in this line of thought, anticipates her role in the distribution of graces deriving from her unique function in the working out of our redemption.

Meditating on these mysteries of faith over the years, I have become a convinced Scotist with regard to the motive of the Incarnation, the Immaculate Conception and the absolute primacy of Christ from which Mary's "subordinate primacy" cannot be separated. At least on the mystery of the Immaculate Conception, St. Thomas' followers have had to concede the point after the solemn definition of the doctrine in 1854, although probably most of them would continue to put up stiff resistance on the other two matters. Nonetheless I continue to believe that these points, so faithfully attested to by Bl. John Duns Scotus and his disciples and so admirably elucidated by Fr. Maximilian in this little book, are not simply the intellectual heritage of Franciscans, but belong to all Christians because they are the teaching that comes to us from the Word of God.

by Monsignor Arthur Burton Calkins, 2006

Preface

While translating a treatise on the Mariology of Blessed John Duns Scotus,[1] it became evident to me that no one would understand Scotus' Mariology well without first understanding his doctrine on the absolute primacy of Christ. And it is this doctrine that answers the most fundamental question, 'Why does Christ exist?' Indeed, Blessed John's doctrine of Christ's primacy is the basis for understanding all Mariology and also, without exaggeration, the ultimate explanation for all of creation, everything that exists outside of God the most Holy Trinity.

Amazingly, in searching for works in the English language on this most important doctrine of the primacy of Christ, I found the resources to be old, scarce, and often too lofty for the average practicing Catholic to understand (or young religious, for that matter). This is ironic in that Bl. John Duns Scotus was from Scotland (hence Scotus) and taught at Oxford and, of course, he was Franciscan. Thus one would expect to find ample materials in English and presentations of this important doctrine in layman's terms since the absolute primacy of Christ is inherently simple!

---

[1] Fr. Ruggero Rosini, OFM, *Mariologia del beato Giovanni Duns Scoto* (Editrice Mariana, Castelpetroso, 1994).

The purpose of this invigorating study of the scotistic doctrine on Christ's absolute predestination to grace and glory is to help the English speaking world, in some small but real way, to encounter firsthand the thought of the Subtle Doctor, Bl. John Duns Scotus. To this end many of the actual writings of Scotus on the subject are included and, with references to the Church Fathers and other reputable theologians, I have commented on these texts in the light of several passages from St. Paul's Epistles in order to underscore the profound insights of Bl. John and draw out some of the implications of this doctrine. I have also included a brief biographical sketch of Scotus' life.

For those who, like myself, are not "professional" theologians in the speculative realm, the present volume will certainly shed new lights on the mystery of Christ Jesus and deepen any reader's love for the Incarnate Word. The topic will be helpful in striving to become better theologians in the contemplative realm (theology, which is the study and knowledge of God, is primarily acquired on one's knees; although the ascetical dimension of intellectual pursuit is indispensable for founding one's devotion upon sound doctrine).

For the theologian this work should suffice as an authentic introduction to the Subtle Doctor's Christology. However, for a more in-depth study in English I would direct you to Fr. Juniper Carol's exhaustive work *Why*

Jesus Christ?[2] and the brief but concentrated synopsis of Fr. Dominic Unger, *Franciscan Christology: Absolute and Universal Primacy of Christ.*[3]

If catechesis means "to reveal in the Person of Christ the whole of God's eternal design reaching fulfillment in that Person,"[4] then pondering the divine plan and purpose in willing the Incarnation will enrich our catechesis and make us more effective evangelists. Since the Church has not definitively made any pronouncement on the primary reason for the Incarnation, she allows and even encourages the faithful to reflect on why God decreed that the Word become flesh. Pondering the divine plan in this way one will find many hints in the Magisterium, since the days of Pope Sixtus IV, responsible in great part for the present liturgy of the Immaculate Conception, that there is much in the deposit of faith to favor the Franciscan thesis. This is particularly the case with the Popes since Bl. Pius IX in the Bull of definition of the Immaculate Conception *Ineffabilis Deus*, Pius XI in the Encyclical *Quas primas* on the absolute Kingship of Christ, Pius XII in the Bull of definition of the Assumption, *Munificentissimus Deus*,

---

2 Fr. Juniper Carol, OFM, *Why Jesus Christ?* (Trinity Communications, Manassas, VA, 1986).

3 Fr. Dominic Unger, OFM Cap., *Franciscan Christology: Absolute and Universal Primacy of Christ*, in FS vol. 22 (N.S. 2) no. 4 (St. Bonaventure, 1942) 428-475.

4 CCC 426.

and in the documents of Vatican II[5], to mention but a few. The Franciscan thesis of the absolute primacy of Christ (versus what is called the thomistic thesis) has innumerable implications which should spark the interest of any true follower of Jesus.

Discovering the primary reason for the Incarnation will affect our view of God: Did He will creation and salvation history in an intelligent, ordered way with Christ as the chief cornerstone? Or did He will one economy of grace for angels and our first parents, and then a better economy of grace in Christ for man as a remedy for sin?

It will affect our view of Jesus and His Mother: Are God's two greatest creative works willed first, before anything else is considered? Are they willed for Their own sake? Do They have priority in the divine scheme of things? Or do the divine Masterpieces of creation owe Their existence to Adam's fall?

It will affect our view of the angels and demons: Did God from all eternity predestine the good angels in, through and for the Incarnate Word—their Mediator of grace and glory—and condemn the demons because they refused to serve the mystery of Christ? Or are the angels created apart from the mystery of the Incarnation and,

---

5 Cf. FR. RUGGERO ROSINI, OFM, *Il Cristocentrismo di G. Duns Scoto e la dottrina del Vaticano II* (Rome, 1967) and his work *Il Cristo nella Bibbia, nei Santi Padri, nel Vaticano II* (Editrice "Esca", Vicenza, 1980).

therefore, not under (at least per se) Christ's headship as the God-Man?

It will affect our view of man: Is the original dignity and sublime calling of man (Adam and Eve included) that of being elevated in Christ Jesus—a predestination of the elect to be God's adopted children in Him, a predestination prior to any consideration of sin? Or could the dignity and predestination of the elect in Christ Jesus be merely a consequence of original sin?

Finally, it will affect our spiritual outlook as well: Did God will from all eternity that man's spiritual journey be centered in the Sacred Hearts of Jesus and Mary, sin or no sin? Or is the sweet journey of the saints to God through Jesus and Mary the result of man's need for redemption?

Please note that throughout this study titles like Jesus, Incarnate Word, Christ, Sacred Heart, Word made flesh, sacred humanity, and God-Man refer to the mystery of the Incarnation and hypostatic union—the union of the two natures of Christ (human nature and divine nature) in the one Person of the Word; when these titles are used they will always refer to the Word as true God and true man. Whereas the titles Eternal Word and Uncreated Word will refer to the Divine Word as such, the second Person of the Blessed Trinity—God from God, Light from Light, true God from true God—with no relation to the mystery of the Incarnation whatsoever.

May the Holy Spirit guide you through these pages for, as our Divine Savior promised,

> *...when He, the Spirit of truth, has come, He will teach you all the truth...He will glorify Me, because He will receive of what is Mine and declare it to you* (Jn. 16:13-14).

Introduction

And the Word was made flesh, and dwelt among us. And we saw His glory—glory as of the only-begotten of the Father—full of grace and truth (Jn. 1:14).

St. John the Evangelist, the disciple whom Jesus loved, relates a fact—*Verbum caro factum est;* the Word was made flesh. We know the fact of the Incarnation (Jn. 1:14) and we know the how—He was conceived by the power of the Holy Spirit and born of the Blessed Virgin Mary (cf. Lk. 1:30-35; Mt. 1:18-25). Our question is not what took place nor how it came about. Our question is '*Why* did it take place at all?'

In reflecting on the reason for the Incarnation, keep in mind that we are not considering a hypothetical question of what might or might not have happened if Adam had not sinned. Rather, faced with the fact of the Incarnation we are seeking—with our human intelligence (philosophy) and through divine revelation (theology)—"*to comprehend with all the saints what is the breadth and length and height and depth, and to know Christ's love which surpasses all knowledge, in order that you may be filled unto all the fullness of God*" (Eph. 3:18-19).

In pondering the primary reason for the Incarnation of the Eternal Word we are joining the company of Apostles, Fathers, Doctors, Saints, theologians, mystics and contemplatives down through the ages who marveled in awe at the God-Man, at *"One like to a Son of Man, clothed with a garment reaching to the ankle, and girt about the breasts with a golden girdle. But His head and His hair were white as wool, and as snow, and His eyes were as a flame of fire, and His voice like the voice of many waters...and His countenance was like the sun shining in its power. And when I saw Him, I fell at His feet as one dead. And He laid His right hand upon me, saying, 'Do not be afraid; I am the First and the Last' "* (Apoc. 1:13-17).

With reverence and love we adore Jesus, true God and true man, and I pray that the *"God of our Lord Jesus Christ, the Father of glory, may grant you the spirit of wisdom and revelation in deep knowledge of Him: the eyes of your mind being enlightened"* (Eph. 1:17-18). The *"mystery of Christ...has been revealed"* (Eph. 3:3-5) and, as the Holy Apostle says, God's *"grace has abounded beyond all measure in us in all wisdom and prudence, so that He may make known to us the mystery of His will according to His good pleasure"* (Eph. 1:8-9).

Chapter 1

Why the God-Man?

In discussing the *raison d'être* of the Incarnation many frequently fall into the hypothetical question, 'If Adam had not sinned, would the Son of God have come in the flesh?' It is important to note that theologians on both sides are asking this question in light of the fact—Christ did indeed come; Christ is our Redeemer. No one is denying the present economy of God's providence; rather, the hypothetical question serves to shed light on the primary reason for the coming of Christ.

Thomistic thesis—no sin, no Incarnation

In general there are only two proposed answers to this question (although there have been attempts at conciliatory answers). On the one hand, there are those who say that the Incarnation is a response to man's sin. According to them the Incarnation is conditional. St. Augustine, Father and Doctor of the Church says, "If man had not sinned, the Son of Man would not have come."[6] Thus 'no sin, no Incarnation.' This position

---

6 St. Augustine, Serm. 174, 2; PL 38, 940.

has come to be known as the thomistic thesis, associated as it is with the great St. Thomas Aquinas who held this position and developed the argument. While St. Thomas wrote that "this is not a very important question"[7] given the actual economy of grace and he himself admits that the opposite "opinion can also be called probable;"[8] nonetheless, he took a definitive stance and this position has borne his name ever since. In his *Summa theologica* he writes that "the work of the Incarnation was ordained by God as a remedy for sin, so that, if sin had not existed, the Incarnation would not have been."[9]

Obviously St. Augustine, St. Thomas and many others answer the hypothetical question thus: the immediate reason for the Incarnation is man's redemption from sin. As St. Ambrose puts it, "What was the cause of the Incarnation if not the redemption of the flesh that had sinned?"[10] The silence of many Fathers on whether 'immediate' is synonymous with 'primary' is not necessarily proof that they held what later came to be known as the thomistic thesis.

Be that as it may, Scripture is replete with apparent affirmations of the thomistic thesis. *"And He hath borne*

---

[7] ST. THOMAS AQUINAS, In 1 Tim., c. 1, lect. 4.

[8] ST. THOMAS AQUINAS, In Sent. III, d. 1, q. 1, a. 3.

[9] ST. THOMAS AQUINAS, *Summa theol. III*, q. 1, a. 3 (Benziger Brothers, NY, 1947) 2028.

[10] ST. AMBROSE, *De Inc. dom. sacram.*, c. 6, n. 56; PL 16, 832.

the sins of many," was Isaias' theme of the Suffering Servant (cf. Is. 53). St. Paul writes to St. Timothy, *"This saying is true and worthy of entire acceptance, that Jesus Christ came into the world to save sinners, of whom I am the chief"* (1 Tim. 1:15). Elsewhere the Apostle writes, *But when the fullness of time came, God sent His Son, born of a woman, born under the Law, to redeem those who were under the Law, that we might receive the adoption of sons* (Gal. 4:4-5). In the letter to the Hebrews it is written, *"But as it is, once for all at the end of the ages, He has appeared for the destruction of sin by the sacrifice of Himself"* (Heb. 9:26).

At this point one might ask, 'Why go on? The answer is crystal clear.' But let us not be too hasty! While the Scriptures clearly state that Jesus Christ came to save sinners, they do *not* state that this is the primary or ultimate reason, let alone the only reason for His coming.

No one denies that redemption from sin is prominent in the Scripture. However, keep in mind that all Sacred Scripture was written *after* original sin. Consequently, our need for redemption is extremely urgent and the remedy for our sin is a most prominent theme throughout. Be that as is it may, the Bible never definitively states that the primary reason of the Incarnation is man's redemption from sin. In fact, as the reader shall see, it strongly suggests just the opposite: the wonder of the redemption is dependent precisely on the prior willing of the Incarnation and is a marvelous manifestation of the absolute predestination of Christ and Mary.

Weaknesses in the thomistic position

Before looking at those who give a resounding 'yes' to the hypothetical question, 'If Adam had not sinned, would Christ have come?', let us briefly expose some of the weaknesses of the thomistic thesis.

First of all, according to the thomistic school, God's two great Masterpieces in creation, namely the Sacred Heart of Jesus and the Immaculate Heart of Mary, are contingent upon sin. Remember, 'no sin, no Incarnation,' and therefore no Mother of God either. Although this sounds radical, it is the logical conclusion. St. Thomas of Villanova (a strict thomist) states plainly that the Blessed Virgin Mary would not have existed if Adam had not fallen.[11] St. Alphonsus holds that Our Lady owes all her grace, glory and dignity to man's fall—without sinners she would never have been worthy of so great a Son."[12]

Further, if man's redemption is the primary reason, then sin has the upper hand. In other words, all the

---

[11] ST. THOMAS OF VILLANOVA, *Sermónes II de la Nativ. de María*; in *Obras de Santo Tomás de Villaneuva*; sermons de la Virgen y obras castellanas (ed. B.A.C., Madrid, 1952) 199.

[12] *St. Alphonsus Liguori, The Glories of Mary*, P. I, c. 6, sect. 2 (ed. by Rev. Eugene Grimm, Brooklyn, 1931) 197; cf. sect. 3, 206-207.

positive blessings of the Incarnation which can be expressed quite apart from redemption would hinge upon sin—our divinization in Christ (2 Cor. 8:9), our adoption as sons of God (cf. Jn. 1:12; Rom. 8:14-17), our eternal predestination in Christ (cf. Rom. 8:29; Eph. 1:3-6), etc. Are all these blessings really because of Adam's fall?

Perhaps the most troublesome aspect of the thomistic thesis is this: St. Paul's insistence on the absolute primacy of Christ. Every Bible-believing Christian must believe in the primacy of Jesus Christ. *"Again, He is the head of His body, the Church; He, who is the beginning, the firstborn of the dead, that in all things He may have the first place"* (Col. 1:18). No one argues against the primacy of God's Son *"come in the flesh"* (1 Jn. 4:2). However, if the Word became flesh only, or even primarily, to redeem man from sin, then His primacy is a *relative primacy*; in other words, the thomists hold that Christ, the end or final cause of all creation, holds primacy only because of Adam's sin. If Adam had not sinned, Christ would not be the end for which all creation exists and the Sacred Heart of Jesus would not even exist! Hence a *relative* primacy (related or linked to sin as its condition).

But St. Paul speaks of an *absolute* primacy of Christ! From all eternity, *"before the foundation of the world"* (Eph. 1:4), God wills the Incarnation absolutely and then, seeing His Masterpiece in creation from all eternity, He wills to create us in, through and unto Him.

*He is the image of the invisible God, the firstborn of
every creature. For in Him were created all things in the
heavens and on the earth...All things have been created
through and unto Him. Again, He is the head of His
body, the Church; He, who is the beginning, the firstborn
of the dead, that in all things He may have the first place*
[primatum tenens] (Col. 1:15-18).

Franciscan thesis—Incarnation, sin or no sin

Now we come full force to the Franciscan, or scotistic
answer to *Cur Deus Homo?*[13] Why the God-Man? Jesus
Christ was absolutely predestined to grace and glory
quite apart from sin, and the elect (both men and angels)
were chosen and predestined in Him by an eternal decree
before the universe had been created (cf. Eph. 1:3-6). St.
Maximus the Confessor writes succinctly,

This is that great and hidden mystery. This is the
blessed end for which all things were created. This is
the divine purpose foreknown before the beginning
of creation...Really, it was for the sake of Christ, that
is the mystery of Christ, that all the ages and all the

---

13 Cur Deus Homo? This is the title of St. Anselm's famous
treatise on the "necessity" of the Incarnation for our redemption.
But in the light of scotistic reflection we might rephrase the
famous title of St. Anselm to read Cur Homo Deus? God did
not primarily become man in order to redeem him in justice,
but rather literally by the Incarnation He made a man God, a
Divine Person capable therefore as man of giving the Father a
maximum possible glory and redeeming the rest of His brethren
in a most perfect way.

things of all the ages themselves received the beginning and end of existence in Christ.[14]

Amongst the greatest minds and most inflamed hearts to deal with this thesis was St. Francis de Sales. He avoided the controversy and with calm precision treated the matter in his *Treatise on the Love of God*. The primary reason for the Incarnation was that God "might communicate Himself" outside Himself (*ad extra*). From all eternity He saw that the most excellent way to do this was in "uniting Himself to some created nature, in such sort that the creature might be engrafted and implanted in the divinity, and become one single Person with it." Thus God willed the Incarnation. Through Christ and "for His sake" God willed to pour out His goodness on other creatures thus choosing to "create men and angels to accompany His Son, to participate in His grace and glory, to adore and praise Him forever."[15]

Another Doctor of the Church, St. Lawrence of Brindisi, expresses it this way:

Therefore, God ordained from all eternity to communicate the infinite treasures of His goodness, to show forth the infinite charity of His mystery by this

---

14 St. Maximus, *Ad Thalassium*, q. 60; PG 90, 620-621.

15 St. Francis de Sales, *Treatise on the Love of God*, Book II, c. 4 (Burns & Oats, 1884—reprinted by TAN, 1997) 73-76.

divine Incarnation in order that Christ might be great and might sit as King at the right hand of God.[16]

And so the scotistic thesis responds to the hypothetical question in the affirmative. St. Mary Magdalen de Pazzi sums it up well: "If Adam had not sinned, the Word would have become incarnate just the same."[17] St. Bernardine of Siena makes it abundantly clear that if Adam sinned, yes, Christ had to become incarnate; "and if he did not sin, He still had to become incarnate: in any hypothesis, He had to become incarnate."[18] And the Venerable Mother Mary of Agreda, marveling at the diversity of opinions in regard to the "principal motive of the Incarnation," received this answer from the Lord,

Know, that the principal and legitimate end of the decree, which I had in view in resolving to communicate My Divinity in the hypostatic union of the Word with human nature, was the glory, which would redound to My name through this communication, and also that which was to redound to the creatures capable

---

16 ST. LAWRENCE OF BRINDISI, "Deus ergo ab aeterno ad communicandos infinitos thesaurus bonitatis suae, ad ostendendam infinitam caritatem suam sacramentum hoc divinae incarnationis ordinavit, ut Christus esset magnus, et sederet rex ad dexteram Dei" in *Mariale*, vol. 1, 81-82 (translation is mine); cf. FR. DOMINIC UNGER, FS vol. 23 (N.S. vol. 2), No. 3 (St. Bonaventure, 1942) 457.

17 ST. MARY MAGDALEN DE PAZZI, *Oeuvres...*, p. 3, c. 3 (trans. from the Italian by A. Bruniaux; Paris, 1873) II, 35.

18 ST. BERNARDINE OF SIENA, *Prediche volgari*, ed. L. Bianchi (Siena, 1888) III, 414-415.

thereof. This decree would without doubt have been executed in the Incarnation, even if the first man had not sinned: for it was an express decree, substantially independent of any condition.[19]

Although our short treatise does not permit an exhaustive dossier of scotists, we do well to mention one more before we move on to Bl. John Duns Scotus himself. St. Albert the Great, Doctor of the Church and interestingly one of St. Thomas Aquinas' professors, humbly held that this position was "more in harmony with the piety of faith." In his commentary on the Sentences he writes,

> to the extent that I can offer my opinion, I believe that the Son of God would have become man even if there had been no sin…Nevertheless, on this subject I say nothing in a definitive manner; but I believe that what I said is more in harmony with the piety of faith.[20]

Ave Maria!

---

19 VEN. MARY OF AGREDA, *City of God*, Book I, c. III, #72-73 (trans. by Fiscar Marison; Corcoran Publishing Co., Albuquerque, 1949) 75-76; cf. Book I, chapters 3-11 (#26-163) which explain the divine decrees regarding Christ and Our Lady.

20 ST. ALBERT THE GREAT, In *sent. III*, d. 20, a. 4; op. omn. ed. Vivès (Paris, 1894) XXVIII, 361.

JOHANNES DUNS SCOTUS

Chapter 2

Blessed John Duns Scotus:
His life[21]

Bl. John Duns Scotus—from Medieval times entitled the *Subtle Doctor* for the acumen and incomparable depth of genius manifested in his doctrine—was born sometime between December, 1265 and March 17, 1266 in Duns in the county of Berwick, Scotland, on the Tweed a few miles from Melrose. The town either gave its name to the family, or the family gave its name to the town. The place of the family home is marked by a monument, and in the public park there is a statue of our Blessed, notwithstanding that Catholics are today a tiny minority in Duns.

John received his first grammar lessons as a young boy at Haddington. During this time he suffered from

---

21 This biographical outline is based largely on the well-documented introduction of FR. DIOMEDE SCARAMUZZI, OFM, in *Duns Scoto Summula: scelta di scritti coordinate in dottrina* (Florence, 1931; reprinted by Libreria Editrice Fiorentina, 1990) and the recent biography of FR. STEFANO MARIA MANELLI, FI, *Beato Giovanni Duns Scoto*, (Frigento, 2005). I have followed Fr. Manelli's accurate summary of the relatively few certain historical facts about the life of Scotus wherever he corrects the affirmations of Fr. Scaramuzzi.

a learning disability. He longed to study and immerse himself in the profound truths of the Faith; but his mind would not cooperate. In this dilemma he had recourse to the Blessed Virgin Mary. He petitioned her with prayers, even tears, that she might assist him. An ancient text reports Our Lady's response to the boy's request:

> O my little devoted one, the prayers and tears which you have offered have pleased me very much. You have led my indulgent Heart to commiserate with your state and console your cries. And see how I am near to you who are so sad in order to grant you every good, according to your desire. Therefore, I shall heal your mental deficiency, and I shall help you with the riches of my Son—not through any merit of yours, but through a heavenly gift…[22]

In 1277 his uncle, Fr. Elias Duns, having recognized John's religious vocation, led him to the friary of the Friars Minor of Dumfries where he himself was Guardian. John received the Franciscan habit as a novice around 1280. He finished his preparatory studies probably at Northampton and Oxford where, according to an ancient Franciscan tradition, he had the celebrated professor Fr. William of Ware, and where one could receive training not only in philosophy and theology, but also in mathematics and the natural sciences. On March 17, 1291, he was ordained a priest by Bishop Oliver Sutton of Lincoln.

---

22 Reported by Fr. Stefano Maria Manelli, FI, in *Beato Giovanni Duns Scoto*, (Frigento, 2005) 11-12.

From 1293 to 1297 he studied at Paris and from 1298 to 1300 he studied at Oxford in order to obtain a higher degree in theology. A noteworthy event took place on Christmas Eve, 1299, at the Friary in Oxford: Fr. John Duns Scotus was immersed in contemplation of the mystery of the Incarnate Word when the Blessed Virgin appeared to him and placed the Infant Jesus in his arms. This grace deeply centered his mind and heart on the mystery of the Incarnation.

In 1300, at Oxford (the most intellectual center of the Franciscan Order, after that of Paris), Scotus commented for the first time on the Sentences of Peter Lombard. In 1302, by order of the Minister General, he returned to Paris and, as a baccalaureate, as was the custom, he commented again upon the Sentences. Between June 25 and 28, 1303, he was obliged to flee Paris because in the fight between Philip the Fair and Pope Boniface VIII he and 86 other friars from that city courageously lined themselves up with the Pope against the King. In this way he gave example of unwavering attachment to the Holy See, whose inviolable rights he defended in his immortal writings, especially his commentary on the Sentences dictated in Paris, which are named *Reportata Parisiensia* (also called *Opus Parisiense*).

During the scholastic year 1303-1304, he taught at the University of Oxford where he wrote what has come to be known as the *Ordinatio* (originally called *Opus*

Oxoniense or *Lectura Oxoniensis*: Oxford work or Oxford Lectures). The title *Ordinatio* indicates that Scotus was giving this set of lectures in theology a definitive order or form, a work left incomplete at his unexpected early death in 1308.

Meanwhile the conflict between France and the Holy See had calmed down and Pope Benedict XI, with a Bull of April 13, 1304, restored the right of the University of Paris to confer degrees—which Boniface VII had taken away August 15, 1303. So Scotus could return to Paris. The Minister General, once a professor at the University, wrote a letter filled with enthusiasm to the Guardian of studies at Paris that he might present Scotus to the University Chancellor for the degree of doctorate and teacher, a degree which Scotus received towards the end of 1305. From 1305 to 1306 he returned to Oxford to teach where he had to defend himself from the vivacious criticisms of the Dominican, Thomas Anglicus. From 1306 to 1307 he was once again at Paris where, according to ancient tradition recorded by Wadding, he taught general Franciscan studies under the title of *Magister regens*. During this last period in Paris he wrote the *Quodlibetum*, according to the testimony of William Alnwick, one of Scotus' disciples.

The fruit of his teaching at Paris was his celebrated *Reportata Parisiensia* (reportage of lectures taken down by the professor's students, hence not directly written by Scotus). Here he defends clearly and vigorously the Immaculate Conception of Mary. This revolutionized the entire University which in the end bowed humbly before the doctrine of this great Franciscan thinker and accepted it. It was Scotus' teaching here that paved the way to the dogmatic definition in 1854 after six centuries of heated debate. According to an ancient and constant Franciscan tradition, Scotus, in the same University, underwent a public dispute regarding the great Marian privilege. In England, Bl. John taught this privilege without opposition; but at Paris the great Masters who preceded him such as Fr. Alexander Hales, St. Bonaventure, and St. Thomas Aquinas, had all taught that Our Lady contracted original sin, even if for just an instant, so as to be redeemed by her Son. When the moment came for him to defend his position against the academic faculty of his day he prayed before a statue of Our Lady saying: "Allow me to praise you, O most Holy Virgin; give me strength against your enemies." She responded visibly, bowing her head slightly before him. In the debate he came out luminously triumphant. Consequently, he has come to be known also as the *Marian Doctor.*

October 25, 1307, Scotus left for Cologne where, according to Mariano of Florence, he was designated lector of theology at the General Chapter of Toulouse, and this appears in the official necrology of that Friary. The inscription written above his tomb—dating back to at least the end of the 14th century—assures that Scotus went to Cologne to combat the error of the Beguardi, (i.e., to deal with the problem of pseudo-mysticism on the rise in the Rhineland, present in some of the condemned propositions of Meister Eckhart, a contemporary of Scotus with whom Scotus together with Fr. Gonsalvus of Spain had debated in Paris. These errors prepared the way for the later rise of the Protestant reformation). Scotus died suddenly at Cologne on November 8, 1308, in the height of his manhood and in the freshness of his energies at the age of 43, surrounded by the immortal halo of sanctity and doctrine.

He was popularly called "blessed" almost immediately after his death, and was so venerated throughout Europe until the Reformation in such widely separated places as Duns, Oxford, Cologne and Nola (an ancient suburb of Naples). The Reformation put an end to that veneration in Duns and Oxford, the French revolution interrupted it in Cologne, but it continued uninterrupted in Nola to the present. Scotus is not well known in lands where the Reformation triumphed, especially in a Calvinistic form, because there every effort was made to eradicate his memory or to remember him only as a fool, whence the origin of the English words "dunce" and "dunce cap" to denote one who stupidly adheres to the doctrines most associated with the name of Scotus as theologian: the absolute primacy of Christ and the mystery of the Eucharist, the Immaculate Conception and the primacy of jurisdiction of St. Peter and his successors in the

Church. These are the points of Catholic doctrine rejected above all in the English version of the Reformation.

The *cultus* of Bl. John Duns Scotus was officially confirmed in St. Peter's Basilica on March 20, 1993, by His Holiness, Pope John Paul II, who dubbed him "the Minstrel of the Word Incarnate" and "Defender of Mary's Immaculate Conception."

Nine years later the Holy Father addressed the Scotus Commission (entrusted with finishing a critical edition of the *Opera Omnia* of Bl. John Duns Scotus), by stressing the importance of scotistic doctrine and underscoring its roots in St. Francis of Assisi and St. Bonaventure. He said,

> Bl. John Duns Scotus is a well-known person in Catholic philosophy and theology, whom my Predecessor Pope Paul VI described in his Apostolic Letter *Alma Parens*, of July 14, 1966, as 'the perfector' of St. Bonaventure, 'the most distinguished representative' of the Franciscan School. On that occasion, Paul VI asserted that in Duns Scotus' writings 'the beautiful form of the perfection of St. Francis of Assisi and the fervor of his seraphic spirit are certainly hidden and yet present.' (cf. AAS 58 [1966] 609-614)...Duns Scotus, with his splendid doctrine on the primacy of Christ, on the Immaculate Conception, on the primary value of the Revelation and of the Magisterium of the Church, on the authority of the Pope, on the

capability of human reason to make the great truths of faith accessible, at least in part, and to show their non-contradictory nature, is even today a pillar of Catholic theology, an original Teacher, full of ideas and incentives for an ever more complete knowledge of the truth of the faith.[23]

Ave Maria!

23 John Paul II, Address to the Members of the Scotus Commission, February 16th, 2002 (from the Vatican website).

Chapter 3

Overview of the scotistic thesis on the primacy of Christ

As we shall see, one of the most beautiful aspects of the Subtle Doctor's teaching on the absolute primacy of Christ is that it begins from above (with God's plan), and not from below (with man's need). Scotus' theology seeks to see the created world from God's point of view, *ad mentem Dei,* and not to subordinate His eternal decrees to man's temporal and spiritual needs. God's works are not conditioned. God is God; then God, in His goodness, freely wills to create the universe according to a fixed plan.

The key to the entire philosophical and theological system of Scotus is *predestination.*[24] This is because for Scotus the origin of all things outside of God hinges entirely on this doctrine. He defines predestination as an "act of the divine will which destines [chooses,

---

24 Cf. Fr. Ruggero Rosini, OFM, *Mariologia del beato Giovanni Duns Scoto*, c. 1, art. 1 (Editrice Mariana, Castelpetroso, 1994) 18-28.

elects] an intellectual creature to grace and glory."[25] This predestination is characterized by two activities, one eternal and the other temporal. The first activity, outside of time, is the intention of God from all eternity. By this is meant the activity of determining the end, the goal, the purpose, the final cause of all God's activity outside Himself (*ad extra*). The second activity is the execution of His foreseen plan in time. By this is meant the gradual realization in time of His eternal purpose.

Intention and execution: we speak here of a single, divine plan of predestination with a twofold activity that brings it about. The first activity (intention) always precedes the second activity (execution). Let us take the example of a sculptor. First, the artisan sees in his mind a life-size wooden statue of the Sacred Heart of Jesus which he wants to carve—so he forms the intention to carve this statue. To execute this foreseen statue he obtains a large chunk of wood, brings the wood to his studio and begins cutting, then whittling away. We see that the process of execution moves from the less perfect (a hunk of wood) to the more perfect (the statue). The sculptor all the while always sees the Sacred Heart of Jesus in that wood and it is this end which moves the execution of the plan along. Thus, in the sculptor's activity of intention the perfect is willed and seen first; whereas in the activity

---

25 BL. JOHN DUNS SCOTUS, *Ordinatio*, I, d. 40, q. 1, n. 4 (Vat. VI, 310).

of execution he begins with the less perfect and gradually moves towards the perfect.

Applying this analogy to the primacy of Christ, God is the Divine Artist. First, He wills and predestines the Most Sacred Heart of Jesus to the maximum grace and glory possible by virtue of the personal union it will have with the Eternal Word in the Incarnation (the hypostatic union). So by the activity of intention God first wills the end of all creation—Jesus Christ. God sets His plan in motion with the creation of the universe moving always from the less perfect towards the most perfect realization of His eternal decree which is the grace and glory of Christ. And so the Sacred Heart is the first created being willed by God—the Alpha—whom God sees from all eternity and predestines to glory, and the Sacred Heart is the goal of all creation—the Omega—which God realizes in the *"fullness of time,"* as St. Paul calls it (Gal. 4:4). This eternal intention of God and temporal execution towards this end is fixed by *predestination*, and all other rational creatures are predestined in, through and unto Christ.

Predestination is a *free act of divine love.* Since predestination is the positive act of the divine will which chooses (elects, destines) a rational creature (namely Christ—and all saints and angels in Him) to grace and glory, it follows that there is a primacy of the will, that is, a primacy of charity in God.[26] This is a keynote of the Franciscan thesis—the primacy of love in God and in His creatures made to His image and likeness. Since predestination is a positive act of the divine will, it is a *free act of love*. Therefore, the cause of all contingent being is rooted in divine charity.

Predestination is *absolute*, not relative or conditional. In other words God predestines Christ (and all angels and men in Him) to grace and glory, not relative to any created need or circumstance, but absolutely. It is God's own intrinsic goodness, His own eternal desire to communicate Himself to another that moves Him to create being outside of Himself (*ad extra*). In other words, God is motivated from within His own Divine Essence to predestine Christ, true God and true man, to the maximum grace and glory; God is not influenced in His freely made, eternal decree by anything extrinsic to Himself. He wills the absolute primacy of Christ unconditionally *"before the foundation of the world."* This means that Jesus Christ is willed for His own sake. He is not willed for man; but men and angels are created for Him and He for God. He is certainly not predestined to grace and glory on account of sin, although He will in His mercy conquer sin. Thus the Incarnation, the

---

26 Cf. the article related to this topic by FR. DOMINIC UNGER, OFM CAP., *The Love of God, the Primary Reason for the Incarnation according to Isaac of Nineveh*, in FS vol. 9, no. 2 (St. Bonaventure, 1949) 146-155.

supreme work of God *ad extra*, is by no means occasioned or brought about by sin.

Finally, predestination is *simultaneous*. With one act of the divine will, God destines all of the elect to grace and glory simultaneously in Christ Jesus. This is illustrated by the joint predestination of Our Lady with Christ. Bl. Pope Pius IX declares in *Ineffabilis Deus* that Mary was predestined to be Mother of God in "one and the same decree" as the Incarnate Word. Men and angels are likewise predestined in this eternal decree as the Holy Apostle Paul indicates (cf. Eph. 1:3-6, 10-11; Col. 1:15-20; Phil. 2:9-11; etc.).

For Scotus, then, all the elect—men and angels— form but one family, the "heavenly court," with Christ Jesus as the Head. Christ is the King of this celestial court with an absolute primacy (and obviously Mary is the Queen, jointly predestined with Him with a subordinate primacy, and we are the adopted children, coheirs with Christ). Christ has absolute primacy because, as Scotus points out, anyone who wills to act does so in an orderly fashion. God is not haphazard in His eternal decrees, but wills in a most orderly fashion, which means He first wills the end, namely the glory of Christ, then that which is closest to this end, namely the Incarnation (which gives grace and glory to Christ), then the divine maternity, then the angels and saints, so that the first place in all the created universe is given to Jesus Christ, King of kings, Lord of lords, Head of the Mystical Body.

Ave Maria!

Chapter 4

Writings of the Subtle Doctor on the absolute primacy of Jesus Christ

From the many writings of Bl. John Duns Scotus there are certain passages which are indispensable for grasping the Franciscan thesis. We report them here without commentary (see the Appendix for the original Latin texts) so that the reader can reflect on his insights firsthand. We will expound his doctrine in the Chapters that follow.

The first text dealing with the primacy is taken from his commentary on the Third Book of Sentences by Fr. Peter Lombard. He wrote or dictated this text during his years as a professor at Oxford (1299-1300) and Paris (1300-1302); it is referred to as the *Ordinatio* (also called *Opus Oxoniense*). The question he introduces before this passage is this: Was Christ predestined to be the Son of God? Once he resolves some objections to Christ's predestination, he writes:

> At this point, however, two questions arise. First, whether this predestination [of Christ] necessarily presupposes the fall of human nature; which is what

many authorities seem to be saying, to the effect that the Son of God would never have become incarnate if man had not fallen.

Without attempting to settle the matter dogmatically, one may state in accord with the last mentioned opinion in distinction 41 of the *First Book* [of Sentences] that, in so far as the objects intended by God are concerned, since the predestination in general of anyone to glory is prior by nature to the prevision of anyone's sin or damnation, this is all the more so true of the predestination of that soul chosen for the greatest glory. For it appears to be universally true that He who wills in an orderly manner intends first that which is nearest the end. And so just as He first intends one to have glory before grace, so also among those predestined to glory, He who wills in an orderly fashion would seem to intend first the glory of the one He wishes to be nearest the end. Thus, He wills glory for this soul before He wills glory for any other soul, and for every other soul He wills glory and grace before He foresees those things which are the opposite of these habits [i.e. sin or damnation]...

If man had not sinned, there would have been no need for our redemption. But that God predestined this soul [of Christ] to so great a glory does not seem to be only on account of that [redemption], since the redemption or the glory of the soul to be redeemed is not comparable to the glory of Christ's soul. Neither is it likely that the highest good in creation is something that was merely occasioned only because of some lesser good; nor is it likely that He predestined Adam to such good before He predestined Christ; and yet this would follow [were the Incarnation occasioned by Adam's sin]. In fact, if the predestination of Christ's soul was for the sole purpose of redeeming others, something even more absurd would follow, namely, that in predestining Adam to glory, He would have foreseen him as having fallen into sin before He predestined Christ to glory.

It can be said, therefore, that with a priority of nature God chose for His heavenly court all the angels and men He wished to have with their various degrees of perfection before He foresaw either sin or the punishment for sinners; and no one has been predestined only because somebody else's sin was foreseen, lest anyone have reason to rejoice over the fall of another.[27]

Another pertinent text from the *Ordinatio*:

I say that the Incarnation of Christ was not foreseen as something occasioned [by sin], but that it was foreseen by God from all eternity and as a good more immediately proximate to the end...Hence this is the order followed in God's prevision. *First*, God understood Himself as the highest good. In the *second*

---

27 BL. JOHN DUNS SCOTUS, *Ordinatio*, III, d. 7, q. 3 (ed. C. Balič, Joannis Duns Scoti, doctoris mariani, theologiae marianae elementa...ad fidem codd. Mss., Sebenici, 1933) 4-7.

instant[28] He understood all creatures. In the *third* He predestined some to glory and grace, and concerning some He had a negative act by not predestining.[29] In the *fourth*, He foresaw that all these would fall in Adam. In the *fifth* He preordained and foresaw the remedy—how they would be redeemed through the Passion of His Son, so that, like all the elect, Christ in the flesh was foreseen and predestined to grace and glory before Christ's Passion was foreseen as a medicine against the fall, just as a physician wills the health of a man before he wills the medicine to cure him.[30]

---

28 Scotus is using human language to communicate priority or order in the divine intentions. God is outside of time and is utterly simple; yet there is an order or priority in His will which Scotus distinguishes with the term "instant." Thomists and scotists alike hold the simplicity of God's decree which has no succession of moments, yet both see a different priority in His willing the Incarnation and Redemption and thus have to communicate this in human terms.

29 "Negative" here means no act on the part of God. God leaves man free—those whom He sees will freely correspond to His gift in Christ and who will persevere to the end will thank Him for His grace; they will thank Him for His positive act of predestination which, with their free cooperation, brought them to Heaven. On the other hand, those who freely reject God's plan and fail to correspond to His calling can only thank themselves in Hell since it was of their own volition. God does not predestine anyone to Hell; rather, seeing their free choice, He omits that positive act of predestination. He forces no one to go to Heaven; He wills no one to go to Hell—seeing from eternity that they will reject His plan He "has a negative act by not predestining them," leaving them free.

30 Bl. John Duns Scotus, *Ordinatio*, III (suppl.), d. 19; cod. Assisi com. 137, fol. 161v.; ed. Vivès (Paris, 1894) XIV, 714.

In his *Opus Parisiense* (or *Reportatio Parisiensis*), he writes:

> It is said that the fall of man is the necessary [in the sense of decisive] reason for this predestination. Since God saw that man would fall, He saw that he would be redeemed in this way, and so He foresaw [Christ's] human nature to be assumed and to be glorified with so great a glory.

> I declare, however, that the fall was not the cause of Christ's predestination. In fact, even if no man or angel had fallen, nor any man but Christ were to be created, Christ would still have been predestined this way. I prove this as follows: because everyone who wills in an orderly manner, wills first the end, then more immediately those things which are closer to the end; but God wills in a most orderly manner; therefore, that is the way He wills. In the first place, then, He wills Himself, and immediately after Him, *ad extra*,[31] is the soul of Christ. Therefore, after first willing those objects intrinsic to Himself, God willed this glory for Christ. Therefore, before any merit or demerit, He foresaw that Christ would be united with Him in the oneness of Person.

---

31 Ad extra, in Trinitarian theology, refers to anything outside of God Himself. Thus everything in the created universe including the sacred humanity of Christ is considered to be extrinsic to the Most Holy Trinity, hence ad extra and not ad intra.

Again, as was declared in the *First Book* (distinction 41) on the question of predestination, the preordination and complete predestination of the elect precedes anything determined concerning the reprobate in fact [*in actu secundo*], lest anyone rejoice over the damnation of another as a benefit to himself. Therefore, the entire process [of predestination] concerning Christ was foreseen prior to the fall and to all demerit.

Again, if the fall were the reason for Christ's predestination, it would follow that the greatest work of God [*summum opus Dei*—namely, the Incarnation] was essentially occasioned: greatest work, because the glory of all creation is not as great in intensity as is the glory of Christ. Hence, it seems very absurd to claim that God would have left so great a work [i.e. the Incarnation] undone on account of a good deed performed by Adam, such as Adam's not sinning.

Therefore, I declare the following: *First*, God loves Himself. *Secondly*, He loves Himself for others, and this is an ordered love. *Thirdly*, He wishes to be loved by Him who can love Him with the greatest love—speaking of the love of someone who is extrinsic to Himself. And *fourthly*, He foresees the union of that nature that must love Him with the greatest love even if no one had fallen.

How, then, are we to understand holy and authoritative writers who say that God would not have been a Mediator unless someone had been a sinner, and many other authorities, who seem to hold the opposite? I hold that glory is ordained for the soul of Christ, and for His body in a manner suitable to the flesh, just as it was granted to His soul when it was assumed. And so too, it [the glory] would have been granted immediately to His body, had this not been delayed on account of the greater good. This was done so that the people could be redeemed from the power of the devil through the Mediator who could and should do so. For the glory of the blessed to be redeemed through the Passion of His body is greater than the glory of Christ's body. Hence, in the *fifth* instant God saw the Mediator coming, suffering and redeeming His people. And He would not have come as a suffering and redeeming Mediator unless someone had first sinned; nor would the glory of the body have been delayed unless there were people to be redeemed. Rather the whole Christ would have been immediately glorified."[32]

In his *Lectura Completa* we read:

Concerning the first question it seems to me that we should answer...if the least of the elect was not predestined because of the fall and reparation of someone else, all the more neither should the predestination of Christ who is the Head of the elect have been occasioned by something like the fall of

---

[32] BL. JOHN DUNS SCOTUS, *Opus Parisiense*, Lib III, d. 7, q. 4 (ed. Balič) 13-15.

the human race. In fact, even if the human race had not fallen, nevertheless He would still have been predestined and His [human] nature united to the Word.[33]

Finally, in the *Reportatio Barcinonensis* he becomes even more emphatic than in the *Ordinatio* when treating of the same subject. Towards the end of his exposition he states:

> Therefore, since the positive act of the divine will regarding the predestined in common precedes all the acts of His will concerning either the reprobate or the fall of anyone whatever, it does not seem that the predestination of Christ to be the Head of the heavenly court was occasioned by the fall or by the demerit of the reprobate. Therefore, God first loves Himself, and nearest in relation to this is his love for the soul of Christ that is to have the greatest glory in the world. And among all created things to be willed, this was first willed—an existence foreseen prior to all merit and hence prior to all demerit.[34]

At first glance, one might not appreciate the depth of insight and ingenious subtlety of the scotistic texts. Bear in mind that before our Blessed no one had ever defended that the Incarnation was not conditioned by sin using

---

33 BL. JOHN DUNS SCOTUS, *Lectura Completa*, III, d. 7, q. 3 (ed. Balič) 188.

34 BL. JOHN DUNS SCOTUS, *Reportatio Barcinonensis*, II, d. 7, q. 3 (ed. Balič) 183-184.

the Scriptural argument of the absolute predestination of Christ and the logical argument that God wills in an orderly fashion. Previous arguments were usually based on fittingness and the rationale that good is diffusive of itself and that love desires to communicate itself to another, hence the hypostatic union.

One might ask: but why then has his thesis come to be known, not as the "scotistic thesis," but the "Franciscan thesis," the *opinio Minorum*, which has been an integral part of Catholic tradition especially since the definition of the Immaculate Conception. Careful study of St. Francis over the past 50 years has shown conclusively that the Poverello of Assisi subscribed both to the thesis on the absolute, joint predestination of Jesus and Mary to be King and Queen of the entire created universe, and to the mystery of the Immaculate Conception under other terms.[35] The original work of Scotus is not the invention of the thesis, but of his translation of St. Francis' contemplative theology into academic terms. This helps us to understand the spirituality of scotists of our day, such as St. Maximilian Mary Kolbe (d. 1941) and the Venerable Fr. Gabriel Allegra (d. 1976). Their spirituality, theologically speaking, rests on these great intuitions of Scotus, but is not for that reason a spirituality less than Franciscan, for the spirituality of St. Francis at its core also

---

35 Cf. Fr. JOHANNES SCHNEIDER, *Virgo Ecclesia Facta: The Presence of Mary in the Crucifix of San Damiano and in the Office of the Passion of St. Francis of Assisi*, (Academy of the Immaculate, New Bedford, 2004).

rests on the mystery of the joint predestination of Jesus and Mary, above all evidenced in the Poverello's perfect conformity to Christ crucified through the maternal mediation of the Immaculate.[36]

In the first text from the *Ordinatio*, notice how Scotus actually skips right over the hypothetical question 'If Adam had not sinned, would Christ have come?' and zooms in on the fact of Christ's predestination to glory:

> Without attempting to settle the matter dogmatically, one may state...that, in so far as the objects intended by God are concerned, since the predestination in general of anyone to glory is prior by nature to the prevision of anyone's sin or damnation, this is all the more so true of the predestination of that soul chosen for the greatest glory.

God predestines the human nature of Christ to the "greatest glory," plain and simple. And just as God freely creates all rational creatures to share in His glory and to be glorified in Him in varying degrees, independently of the prevision of sin, how much more so the sacred humanity of Christ! The human nature of the God-Man was chosen to be the creature most perfectly glorified by the Blessed Trinity and to render the most perfect glory to God in the created universe.

---

36 Cf. FR. PETER MARY FEHLNER and FR. MAXIMILIAN MARY DEAN, *Virgo Facta Ecclesia: The Marian life and charism of St. Francis of Assisi*, (Academy of the Immaculate, New Bedford, 1997).

Our Blessed writes,

> It can be said that with a priority of nature God chose
> for His heavenly court all the angels and men He wished
> to have with their various degrees of perfection before
> He foresaw sin or the punishment for sinners; and no
> one has been predestined only because somebody else's
> sin was foreseen, lest anyone have reason to rejoice over
> the fall of another.[37]

Stated positively, God predestines Christ, saints and angels
to grace and glory before any foreseen sin. Predestination
is absolute in the intention of God and not relative to
the foreseen needs of creatures. Scotus holds that this
is true especially in the case of the God-Man. To say
that the predestination of Christ's soul was exclusively
for redeeming others from sin was for Scotus "absurd."
Christ's absolute predestination was not "occasioned"
by sin or any lesser good that might accrue to men and
angels.

Ave Maria!

---

[37] Bl. John Duns Scotus, *Ordinatio* d. 7, q. 3.

Chapter 5

Scriptural Foundations

At this point we do well to look at the Scriptural foundations for Scotus' doctrine on the absolute primacy of Christ. The three key passages are found in St. Paul's Epistles. The first is the Canticle in the Epistle to the Ephesians which Holy Mother Church chants every week in the Liturgy of the Hours of the Roman Rite (Monday, Evening Prayer).

A. Ephesians 1:3–10

v.3 *Blessed be the God and Father of our Lord Jesus Christ, who has blessed us with every spiritual blessing on high in Christ.*

v.4 *Even as He chose us in Him before the foundation of the world, that we should be holy and without blemish in His sight in love.*

v.5 *He predestined us to be adopted through Jesus Christ as His sons, according to the purpose of His will,* v.6 *unto the praise of the glory of His grace, with which He has favored us in His beloved Son.*

v.7 *In Him we have redemption through His blood, the remission of sins, according to the riches of His grace.*

v.8 *This grace has abounded beyond measure in us in all wisdom and prudence,*

v.9 *so that He may make known to us the mystery of His will according to His good pleasure. And this His good pleasure He purposed in Him*

v.10 *to be dispensed in the fullness of the times: to re-establish all things in Christ, both those in the heavens and those on the earth.*

Verses 3-6, absolute predestination

In verses 3-6, St. Paul could not be clearer—in God's eternal design, *"before the foundation of the world,"* He has first predestined Christ to glory then, *"in Him"* He has predestined the elect to be His adopted children *"according to the purpose of His will."* The predestination of Jesus Christ and the predestination of the elect in Him is absolute and the primary blessings of this are to *"be holy and without blemish in His sight in love…to be adopted sons…unto the praise of the glory of His grace, with which He has favored us in His beloved Son."*

By virtue of the divine decree, Jesus is the perfect Glorifier of God *ad extra* and Jesus is the creature most perfectly glorified by God; the elect, by virtue of their predestination in Him, glorify God and are blessed by the Lord *"with every spiritual blessing on high in Christ."* Here we see the primary reason for God's free, creative act—*grace and glory.* Notice that there is no mention of sin in these verses.

Verse 7, Christ as Redeemer

Like St. Paul, neither Scotus nor the Franciscan school deny or downplay the coming of Christ as Redeemer. Far from it! Rather they underscore not simply the character of that redemption as satisfaction of divine justice, but why in the first place such a mode of redemption should have been chosen by the Father, and why it is the most perfect among possible solutions, a perfection and superabundance (cf. Rom. 5:12 ff.). Even the Immaculate Conception, according to the Subtle Doctor, is the "perfect fruit of a perfect redemption by a perfect Redeemer."[38] Hence, when we add to the absolute predestination of Christ to grace and glory His work of redemption, we add a most precious jewel in His royal crown. For, as the Apostle goes on to say in the next verse, *"in Him we have redemption through His blood, the remission of sins, according to the riches of His grace"* (Eph.

---

[38] BL. JOHN DUNS SCOTUS, *Ordinatio,* III, d. 3.

1:7). After the fall of our first parents, we are unable to benefit from the Incarnation of the Word unless we are first redeemed. The saints from the time of Adam on, although predestined in Christ Jesus, find themselves cut off from grace by sin and deserving of the punishment due to sin. They were *"dead"* by reason of their offenses and sins, *"children of wrath." "But God, who is rich in mercy, by reason of His very great love wherewith He has loved us even when we were dead by reason of our sins, brought us to life together with Christ..."* (cf. Eph. 2:1-10).

Jesus Christ indeed came into this world to redeem man from sin. However, nowhere in Scripture does it say that He came primarily, let alone exclusively, for the redemption. In fact, it is the Sacred Page which tells us of the many other blessings bestowed through the Incarnation: filial adoption (Eph. 1:5; Gal. 4:5; etc.); deification (2 Pt. 1:4; 2 Cor. 8:9); enlightenment (Jn. 1:9); revelation of the Father (Mt. 11:27; Jn. 1:18; 12:45; 14:9), etc.

Franciscans have always been preachers of *"Jesus Christ and Him crucified"* (1 Cor. 2:2). After all, their Founder and spiritual Father St. Francis of Assisi bore the wounds of Christ in his body. Moreover, his sons who have been caring for the sacred places in the Holy Land since the 14th century have spread everywhere the devotion to the Stations of the Cross, so much so that hardly a chapel in the world is without them.

Belief in the absolute primacy of Christ underscores that God did not send His Son as an afterthought, as a consequence of sin, as if sin made the Incarnation necessary. No, God sent His Son *"by reason of His very great love"* (Eph. 2:4). God freely and eternally decreed the blessings of the Incarnation for Christ and, in Him and through Him, for all the elect. Sin or no sin, Jesus Christ was predestined and the elect in Him; because of man's sin, however, the most salient feature of the Incarnate Word's earthly life was His redemptive Passion. If Adam had not sinned, Christ would not have had to shed His Precious Blood; neither would His Immaculate Mother have had to endure the sword of sorrow, but more on that later.

Christ came "for our salvation"

It is worth noting that the Nicene Creed, after professing the Divinity of the Eternal Son of God, declares: "For us men and for our salvation He came down from Heaven." Three distinctions need to be made here. First, those holding to the absolute primacy of the Word made flesh never deny that our Lord and Savior Jesus Christ came to redeem us. He comes as Redeemer; but this is not the *primary* reason God wills the Incarnation. Christ is willed first for His own sake, for the glory He will give to the Father in Himself; then, secondarily, He is willed for our redemption. Thus the absolute primacy of Christ acknowledges that Christ came for man's redemption secondarily.

Secondly, as St. Irenaeus (d. 190) points out,[39] "redemption" and "salvation" are not synonyms. Since the Scriptures are written after the fall, there is no question that salvation *from sin* (redemption) is emphasized. But a careful reading of the Epistle to the Romans shows that salvation has a much broader meaning. It refers to being justified through faith. A person who is justified by faith is saved; he is transformed from within by sanctifying grace. In the case of fallen man it is a salvation which transforms one from being in a state of sin into being in a state of grace: *"So that as sin has reigned unto death, so also grace may reign by justice unto life everlasting through Jesus Christ our Lord."* (Rom. 5:21). But the state of grace is first and foremost an ontological elevation for man. Apart from sin, to be justified, to be saved, means to be elevated or transformed from being a mere natural creature into being a *"new creation,"* a supernatural creature able to call God *"Abba Father"*! Salvation from sin is part of this ontological elevation which remedies our moral deficiency after the fall; however, "our salvation" is primarily what the Church Fathers call divinization or deification—to become, as St. Peter puts it, *"partakers of the divine nature"*

---

39 Cf. Fr. DOMINIC UNGER, OFM CAP., *Christ's Role in the Universe according to St. Irenaeus*, in FS 26 (1945) 3-20, 114-137.

(2 Pt. 1:4).[40] And it is St. Peter who emphasizes that there is salvation in no other name under Heaven but Jesus Christ (cf. Acts 4:8-12).

Thirdly, redemption is not restricted simply to liberating one from sin, but can also refer to preventing one from contracting original sin or committing actual sin. This is precisely the case with the Immaculate Virgin Mary—she is the perfect fruit of a perfect redemption wrought by a perfect Redeemer.[41] Hers is a preservative redemption; ours a liberative redemption. St. Lawrence of Brindisi held that if Adam had not sinned, Christ could have come as Savior with preventative medicine instead of a remedy for sickness already contracted. It can be argued that the good angels received the grace to serve Him and the preventative medicine not to sin from His coming as Savior. In fact, Savior (*soter*) primarily connotes one who preserves. In the Old Testament, for example, Joseph was

---

[40] The theology of deification or divinization in Christ is considered one of the chief contributions of St. Athanasius, cf. FR. DOMINIC UNGER, OFM CAP., *A Special Aspect of Athanasian Soteriology—Part I*, in FS vol. 6, no. 1 (1946) 30-53; cf. also FR. UNGER'S treatment of St. Cyril of Alexandria in this regard, *Christ Jesus the Secure Foundation—According to St. Cyril of Alexandria—Part I*, in FS vol. 7 (1947) 18-25.

[41] Cf. BL. JOHN DUNS SCOTUS, *Ordinatio*, III, d. 3; cf. also FR. PETER FEHLNER, FI, *The Sense of Marian Coredemption in St. Bonaventure and Bl. John Duns Scotus*, in *Mary at the Foot of the Cross* (Academy of the Immaculate, New Bedford, 2001) 103-118.

called *"Savior of the world"* because he preserved everyone from famine (Gen. 41:45).[42]

Verses 8-9, the mystery of His will

St. Paul, after mentioning the redemption in his Canticle, continues:

> *This grace has abounded beyond measure in us in all wisdom and prudence, so that He may make known to us the mystery of His will according to His good pleasure. And this His good pleasure He purposed in Him to be dispensed in the fullness of times: to re-establish* [the Greek reads "to sum up under one heading"] *all things in Christ, both those in the heavens and those on earth* (Eph. 1:8-10).

St. Paul speaks of a hidden mystery:

> *Yes, to me, the very least of all the saints, there was given this grace... to enlighten all men as to what is the dispensation of the mystery which has been hidden from eternity in God who created all things; in order that through the Church there be made known to the Principalities and the Powers in the heavens the manifold wisdom of God according to the eternal purpose which He accomplished in Christ Jesus our Lord* (Eph. 3:7-11).

---

42 Cf. ST. LAWRENCE OF BRINDISI, *Mariale*, vol. 1, p. 86; cf. FR. DOMINIC UNGER, OFM CAP., *Franciscan Christology: Absolute and Universal Primacy of Christ*, in FS vol. 22 (N.S. 2) no. 4 (1942) 461.

This mystery was first made known to St. Paul by revelation (cf. Eph. 3:3-5). It is *"the mystery which has been hidden for ages and generations"* (Col. 1:26). *"But we speak of the wisdom of God, mysterious, hidden, which God foreordained before the world unto our glory."* (1 Cor. 2:7).

What is this mystery? St. Maximus the Confessor, a prominent Greek Father of the Church (d. 662), comments on this. Christ, the Word made flesh,

> is that great and hidden mystery. This is that blessed end for which all things were created. This is the divine scope foreknown before the beginning of creatures, which we define to be the end that was foreknown, on account of which all things [exist], but itself [exists] on account of nothing. With this end in view God produced the essences of creatures. This is properly the end of providence and of the things foreknown...this is the mystery that contains all the ages and that manifests the great plan of God which is infinite and pre-existed the ages, and the things in the ages themselves received the beginning and the end of existence in Christ...This [hypostatic union] was made when Christ appeared in the last times. By itself it is the fulfillment of the foreknowledge of God.[43]

---

[43] ST. MAXIMUS, *Ad Thalassium*, q. 60; PG 90; 620-621; Cf. FR. DOMINIC UNGER, OFM CAP., *Christ Jesus, Center and Final Scope of all Creation According to St. Maximus Confessor*, in FS vol. 9, no. 1 (1949) 50-62.

This mystery, namely the Incarnation of the Eternal Son of God, is made known to us "in the last times," as St. Maximus puts it referring to the expression in the Epistle to the Hebrews (1:2; cf. 1 Pt. 1:20); but St. Paul also refers to it more exquisitely as the *"fullness of times"* (Eph. 1:10), an expression he uses also in Galatians 4:4 where he speaks of God sending His Son, born of a woman, that we might receive the adoption of sons. Indeed if God's eternal decree was the absolute primacy of Jesus Christ, then the Incarnation and birth of Jesus is truly the *"fullness of times."* All of creation, all of history, points to Christ the King and exists for Him.

Verse 10, the headship of Christ

At this point in the Canticle, St. Paul himself proclaims the mystery: *"to re-establish all things in Christ, both in the heavens and those on the earth."* (Eph. 1:10). Sadly the Latin and many English translations are rendered differently than Paul's original Greek. In fact, St. Jerome in translating the Bible into Latin was surprised at the word *instaurare* (restore, re-establish, reconcile) found in other Latin translations of the passage during his time. However, because this translation was already well-known to Latin-speaking Christians, he opted to leave it as is.[44] The Greek word *anakephalai sasthei* means "to sum up under one heading." Thus a more literal translation might

---

[44] St. Jerome, In *Eph. ad Eph.*, I, 1, 10; PL 26, 483

read, *"And this His good pleasure He purposed in Him to be dispensed in the fullness of times:* to sum up all things under the headship of Christ, *both in the heavens and those on the earth."* This is a clear assertion of the absolute primacy of Christ over men and angels, a theme that we will treat more at length when we look at the Epistle to the Colossians.

Although we have finished examining this passage, we do well to note what the Apostle adds in the next verse,

> *In Him, I say, in whom we also have been called by a special choice, having been predestined in the purpose of Him who works all things according to the counsel of His will, to contribute to the praise of His glory* (Eph. 1:11-12).

God's purpose, then, is the absolute predestination of Christ to grace and glory, and in Him, by *"a special choice,"* the elect are *"predestined...to contribute to the praise of His glory."*

B. Romans 8:29

Continuing with the theme of predestination, we move on to a short, but enlightening verse—Romans 8:29. We quote it in its context:

v.28 *Now we know that for those who love God all things work together unto good, for those who according to His purpose, are saints through His call.*

v.29 *For those whom He has foreknown He has also predestined to become conformed to the image of His Son, that He should be the firstborn among many brethren.*

v.30 *And those whom He has predestined, them He has also called; and those whom He has called, them He has also justified, and those whom He has justified, them He has also glorified.*

His purpose

We recall that predestination consists in a twofold divine activity. The first activity is the intention or *"purpose"* of God which is eternal, before anyone or anything exists; the second activity is the realization of that purpose in time by way of execution. The Apostle first mentions that the elect, that is, the saints, are chosen according to God's purpose through His call. In explaining predestination, Bl. John Duns Scotus refers to the principle of Aristotle:

"What is first in intention is last in execution."[45] This is precisely what the Apostle reveals—first God forms the intention, He has a purpose from all eternity, and then all things in the order of creation flow according to His plan, which is the execution.

Based on this passage of St. Paul, what is the divine intention? *"For those whom He has foreknown He has also predestined to become conformed to the image of His Son."* (Rom. 8:29). Before God creates, calls, justifies, and glorifies His saints, He *predestines* them to be *"conformed to the image of His Son."* This necessarily means that God predestined and foresaw Jesus Christ, the Word Incarnate, first in His plan. The sacred humanity of Christ is predestined to grace and glory and the saints are predestined *in Him*.

Conformed to whom?

Some have objected that St. Paul might only be speaking here of the Son of God as the Eternal, Uncreated Word and that the elect are predestined from eternity *"to become conformed to the image of the Son"* apart from the Incarnation. There are two problems with this interpretation. First of all, why specifically a predestination to be conformed *to the Son* and not the whole Trinity? Since the Uncreated Word is "God from God, Light from Light, true God from true God, begotten

---

45 ARISTOTLE, *Metaphysica*, VI, t. 7, c. 23

not made, one in being with the Father," it makes more sense that St. Paul is referring to the Word *Incarnate*. In fact, throughout the entire eighth chapter of his Epistle he refers only to Christ, the Word Incarnate, and never to the Uncreated Word as such. This is confirmed elsewhere when the Apostle speaks clearly of predestination in Christ Jesus,

> *according to His own purpose and the grace which was granted to us in Christ Jesus before this world existed, but is now made known by the manifestation of our Savior Jesus Christ* (2 Tim. 1:9-10).

Therefore, the Franciscan school maintains that the elect are predestined to be conformed to the Son precisely because God first sees His Son *incarnate*, He sees the love burning in the most Sacred Heart of Jesus from all eternity, and then He freely chooses to create and conform His saints to the image of His Son who is *"the brightness of His glory and the image of His substance."* (Heb. 1:3).

The second problem entailed in interpreting this passage only in reference to the Eternal Word is simply that Paul himself indicates the contrary. If the elect are predestined to be conformed to the image of the Son, it is so *"that He should be the firstborn among many brethren."* Jesus is our brother precisely as the Son of Man, and not as the Uncreated Word. And along with this short clarification we also see that *man exists for Christ*, man is predestined in Him so that He might have the absolute primacy. He is the *"firstborn,"* not chronologically, but in the mind of God. God sees the Heart of Christ first, then He sees angels and men in Him who is the *"firstborn"* in the intention of God, but who comes *"last of all in these days"* in the order of execution (cf. Heb. 1:2).

Absolute predestination of Christ

Having established the predestination of Christ to grace and glory and the predestination of the saints in Him from Sacred Scripture, we can now appreciate more fully the convincing observations of the Subtle Doctor. In his *Opus Parisiense* he writes:

> It is said that the fall of man is the necessary reason for this predestination [of Christ]. Since God saw that man would fall, He saw that He would be redeemed in this way, and so He foresaw [Christ's] human nature to be assumed and to be glorified with so great a glory.

> I declare, however, that the fall was not the cause of Christ's predestination. In fact, even if no man or angel had fallen, nor any man but Christ were to be

created, Christ would still have been predestined in this way...[46]

Before continuing with his proof for this, we note how the predestination of the sacred humanity of Christ to glory through the personal union with the Eternal Word in the Incarnation is not conditioned by anything created, nor by any good or evil act that might be committed by a creature. Christ is predestined absolutely, *a parte rei*. In fact, "if the fall were the reason for Christ's predestination," Scotus later writes, "it would follow that the greatest work of God [the Incarnation] was essentially occasioned." To say that the *summum opus Dei*, the greatest work of God was occasioned by a lesser good, or worse, by an evil act committed by a lesser creature, seems outrageous! No, Jesus Christ is the first one predestined and this for His own sake, namely to be that creature most perfectly glorified by God and to be that creature to adore Him most perfectly. To say

---

46 BL. JOHN DUNS SCOTUS, *Opus Parisiense*, Lib III, d. 7, q. 4. This point is further elaborated by Scotus' critique of St. Anselm's position on the relation between an Incarnation motivated primarily by the fall of Adam and therefore the need of a Redeemer both divine and human and so capable of condign satisfaction for sin. The thesis of St. Anselm provides an essential premise for both the soteriology of St. Bonaventure and that of St. Thomas. Bl. John Duns Scotus locates the primary motive of the Incarnation in something prior to sin, and so is able to establish principles which show why a redemption entailing just satisfaction occasioned by the sin of Adam was in fact chosen in view of the prior, absolute, joint predestination of the Incarnation of the Word and of His Immaculate Mother. Cf. *Lectura III*, d. 20.

that God's Masterpiece in all creation is subordinated to some secondary end or that He is occasioned by the fall of Adam is nonsensical.

To use a simple analogy, we say that "the dog is man's best friend," clearly connoting that the lesser being, the dog, is ordered to the higher being, man. No one would say "man is the dog's best friend," as if the free, rational human being exists primarily for the canine. Although a dog may benefit from his owner, the owner does not exist primarily for his pet. Similarly, we exist for Christ, not He for us. *"For if we live, we live to the Lord."* (Rom. 14:8); *"you are Christ's, and Christ is God's"* (1 Cor. 3:23). And although we can benefit from belonging to Christ, nonetheless, He does not exist primarily for us, but we for Him.

Scotus describes the hypostatic union as the greatest work of God

…because the glory of all creation is not as great in intensity as is the glory of Christ. Hence, it seems very absurd to claim that God would have left so great a work [i.e. the Incarnation] undone on account of a good deed performed by Adam, such as Adam's not sinning.[47]

---

47 Ibid.

The proof of Scotus

Now the Subtle Doctor proves the absolute predestination of Christ in this way:

> I prove this as follows: because everyone who wills in an orderly manner, wills first the end, then more immediately those things which are closer to the end; but God wills in a most orderly manner; therefore, that is the way He wills. In the first place, then, He wills Himself, and immediately after Him, *ad extra*, is the soul of Christ. Therefore, after first willing those objects intrinsic to Himself, God willed this glory for Christ. Therefore, before any merit or demerit, He foresaw that Christ would be united with Him in the oneness of Person.[48]

Just as an architect wills first the building, then those things closest to the end (i.e. the interior design, the insulation, electricity, plumbing, roof, frame, foundation, etc.); so God, the Divine Architect of the universe, first wills "those objects intrinsic to Himself," then that which is closest to the end, "the soul of Christ." First, God exists in Himself—One in Essence, Three in Persons—then He wills that which is closest to Himself *ad extra*, namely Jesus Christ, then His Immaculate Mother, then the angels and men, then the natural universe.

---

48 Ibid.

For our Blessed this logically proves Christ's absolute primacy over all creation. Otherwise, one would have to conclude that God wills in a disorderly fashion. While God is free, no one denies that God cannot do what is metaphysically impossible. Based on this axiom, it would be a contradiction for God to will in a disordered way— namely to will His greatest work because of Adam's sin.

The Incarnation is a pure gift of Love

Scotus emphasizes that "before any merit or demerit, He [God] foresaw that Christ would be united with Him in the oneness of Person."[49] The Incarnation is the one completely gratuitous gift of God to a creature apart from any merit or demerit. All other gifts of God are merited by Christ Himself or by others united to Him, so that even the Immaculate Conception of Mary, although not merited by her, was given to her by virtue of the foreseen merits of Christ. But the grace and glory given to the sacred humanity of Jesus by virtue of the hypostatic union are a free, gratuitous gift of God who is Himself Love. This gift of grace and glory to the human nature of Jesus, foreordained by God, was a pure gift. It was not given based on anyone's merit and certainly not on account of anyone's demerit.

In fact, the predestination of each of the elect to glory precedes any liberation from the loss of that glory through

---

49 Ibid.

sin. Otherwise, the saints would rejoice over another's fall. The Subtle Doctor puts it this way,

> The preordination and complete predestination of the elect precedes anything determined concerning the reprobate in fact, lest anyone rejoice over the damnation of another as a benefit to himself.

If the Sacred Heart of Jesus was predestined to the highest glory solely or primarily because of Adam's sin, then He Himself would owe a debt of gratitude to Adam for falling. "Therefore," Scotus finishes, "the entire process concerning Christ was foreseen prior to the fall and to all demerit."[50]

"O happy fault"?

On this note, however, we must contend with an impelling objection that might seem to undo all that we have been saying. There is a saying in the Church that goes like this, *lex orandi, lex credendi,* the norm of prayer is the norm of faith. In other words, as the Church prays so she believes—her prayers indicate her Creed. Now every year at the Easter Vigil there is sung with fervent joy in Catholic churches throughout the world the *Exultet* written by St. Ambrose (d. 397). In the last half of that triumphant hymn the cantor sings, "What good would life have been to us, had Christ not come as

---

50 Ibid.

our Redeemer?" Then, a few lines later, "O happy fault, O necessary sin of Adam, which gained for us so great a Redeemer!" These are troublesome lines to the scotist, to say the least! However, this is not a closed case for the thomistic thesis; some observations must be made.

First, notice that these lines speak of a *Redeemer*. Nowhere does it say that sin was necessary for the Incarnation, or that Adam's fall occasioned the eternal predestination of Christ. Simply put, if Adam had not sinned Christ would not have come *as Redeemer* and so the sin of Adam can be said to be necessary if Christ is to come as our Redeemer. 'No sin, no Redeemer'; but it does not follow 'no sin, no Incarnation.' Also, the scotist acknowledges that after the fall life would not be good to us at all without the Redeemer.

Moreover, is holy Mother Church inviting us to rejoice in Adam's fall? "O *happy* fault"!?! I respond in the negative, and for two reasons. First of all, this is a poetic hymn praising God for the victory of Christ's resurrection from the dead. For example, the earth is invited to "rejoice"—obviously a poetic expression.[51] The cantor speaks of this night being chosen by God "to see" the Resurrection—poetic in that night cannot

---

[51] On a deeper level this line echoes biblical typology, where "virgin earth" is a type of the Virgin Mary by whom Christ in His human nature was formed, as the first Adam was formed by God from the "virgin earth," hence, the earth here alludes to the joy of Our Lady, and all united to her, at the Resurrection.

"see." And so we take the *Exultet* for what it is, a poetic Easter proclamation of joy and victory. Besides, to be happy and rejoice at another's fall would be a sin against charity. Certainly the Church is not exulting in Adam's wicked deed, but rejoicing in God's victory over sin through the Paschal mystery. In the final analysis, a scotistic Franciscan even more will sing out the *Exultet* at the Easter Vigil with great jubilation and still hold tenaciously to the absolute primacy of Christ the King. For it is this very primacy which accounts for our good fortune, despite the apparently definitive success of the serpent and irreversible character of the original disaster. "O happy fault," not because it caused the Incarnation, but because God in His mercy willed to remedy our woe in such a perfect way. The Church, then, is not declaring a relative primacy of Christ in the *Exultet*, but rather, she is rejoicing wholeheartedly in Christ the King's victorious resurrection from the dead.

C. Colossians 1:15–20

Now we come to what is perhaps the most significant scriptural text on the absolute primacy of Christ: St. Paul's Canticle in his Epistle to the Colossians. Before he begins this Canticle the Apostle remarks that he has been praying for the Colossians, *"asking that you may be filled with knowledge of His will, in all spiritual wisdom and understanding."* (Col. 1:9). May the Apostle intercede and obtain this grace for us as well!

In this Canticle we will see an undaunted profession of the *primacy of Christ*. Scotists, thomists, and all other Bible-believing Christians will agree that Christ has the primacy. But is it a *relative* primacy contingent on sin? Or is it an *absolute* primacy? We believe that this Pauline text reveals the primacy of Christ to be absolute.

v.15 *He is the image of the invisible God, the firstborn of every creature.*

v.16 *For in Him were created all things in the heavens and on the earth, things visible and things invisible, whether Thrones, or Dominations, or Principalities, or Powers. All things have been created through and unto Him,*

v.17 *and He is before all creatures, and in Him all things hold together.*

v.18 *Again, He is the head of His body, the Church; He, who is the beginning, the firstborn from the dead, that in all things He may have the first place.*

v.19 *For it has pleased God the Father that in Him all fullness should dwell,*

v.20 *and that through Him He should reconcile to Himself all things, whether on the earth or in the heavens, making peace through the blood of His Cross.*

Who is the subject of the Canticle?

In St. Paul's Epistle to the Romans we discussed the Apostle's use of the words *"image"* and *"firstborn"* in reference to the Incarnate Word. These themes carry over into our study of the Apostle's Canticle in the Epistle to the Colossians which the Church chants weekly in her Liturgy of the Hours of the Roman Rite (Wednesday, Evening Prayer).

In verses 13 and 14 which precede this Canticle the Holy Apostle writes that God *"has rescued us from the power of darkness and transferred us into the kingdom of His beloved Son, in whom we have our redemption, the remission of our sins. He is the image of the invisible God, the firstborn of every creature..."*

The key here is this: who is the subject in the Apostle's Canticle? If it is Jesus Christ, the Incarnate Word, as is indicated before the Canticle in verses 13 and 14 (*"His beloved Son in whom we have our redemption"*) and at the conclusion of the Canticle in verse 20 (*"His Cross"*), then we have a clear profession of the absolute primacy of Christ.

First of all, the passage appears as a unified whole without transition. There is no sign from Paul that the one *"in whom we have our redemption"* is different than the *"He"* who is *"the image of the invisible God, the firstborn of every creature…"* Thus the subject is always Christ *"come in the flesh"* (1 Jn. 4:18).

Secondly, the Apostle is writing to the Colossians who were invoking the angels, like Platonic demiurges, as intermediaries between God and man. Their error was a denial of the absolute primacy of the God-Man over and above the angels. Hence St. Paul writes of Christ, *"For in Him dwells all the fullness of Godhead bodily, and in Him who is the head of every Principality and Power you have received of that fullness."* (Col. 2:9-10). Clearly, then, Paul is referring to the Word Incarnate, in whom *"dwells all the fullness of Godhead bodily."* Paul is not shifting in the middle of his Canticle from the Word Incarnate to the Eternal, Uncreated Word, and then switching back at the end to the Word Incarnate. No, his pastoral and doctrinal concern with the Colossians deals entirely with the supremacy of Jesus Christ, the *"one mediator between God and man, Himself a man, Christ Jesus."* (1 Tim. 2:5).

Finally, the two words *"image"* and *"firstborn"* in verse 15 refer here, as in Romans 8:29, to the Word made flesh. This is the opinion of St. Athanasius, St. Gregory of Nyssa, St. Jerome, St. Cyril of Alexandria, St. Bede and many others long before the Franciscan school existed; this is also stated clearly by Pope Benedict XVI in his *General Audience* of January 4, 2006:

> Dear Brothers and Sisters in Christ, in this first General Audience of the New Year, we reflect on the famous Christological hymn from the Letter to the Colossians. It sets a tone of thanksgiving for these first days of the year two thousand and six. Christ is at the centre of this hymn. He is presented to us as the first-born of all creation, the image of the invisible God. The expression 'image', like an Eastern icon, indicates more than a likeness, it brings out the profound intimacy that exists with the subject that is represented.
>
> Christ is also portrayed as Redeemer, within the vast sweep of salvation history. As Head of His body, the Church, He is joined in communion with all her members, living and dead, and He opens for us the way to eternal life. The fullness of grace that we receive

from Him transforms us within, so that we become sharers in His divinity.[52]

Benedict XVI here asserts that Christ, the Word Incarnate, is the subject of the entire Canticle. It is Jesus Christ who is *"image of the invisible God"* and *"firstborn of all creation."* Let us examine these points more deeply.

Verse 15, image of the invisible God

"He is the image of the invisible God." We know that within the Trinity the Uncreated Word eternally proceeds from the Father as His perfect image. But our Apostle is not referring to the eternal generation of the Son from the Father; rather, he is referring to the image of *the invisible Godhead*, not the image of the Father. The Eternal Word is not the image of the invisible Godhead because He Himself is the invisible God—"God from God, Light from Light, true God from true God…one in being with the Father." Furthermore, the Apostle indicates by the word *"invisible"* that this *"image of the invisible God"* is a visible image; otherwise the verse makes no sense. So he is referring to the Word Incarnate as the visible image of the invisible God. In describing to the Corinthians the Gospel he preaches and mentioning those who are perishing, he adds: *"In their case, the god of this world has blinded their unbelieving minds, that they should not see the light of the*

---

52 Pope Benedict XVI, General Audience (January 4, 2006) Vatican website.

Gospel of the glory of Christ, who is the image of God" (2 Cor. 4:4). Notice who the image of God is—Christ!

The Greek word that is translated 'image' is *eikon.* Since we are familiar with icons in the Eastern Churches, perhaps Paul's meaning is more clear if we translate *"He is the image of the invisible God"* as, "He is the icon (*eikon*) of the invisible God." Now an icon implies two things. The first is representation. In this case the sacred humanity of Christ re-presents to us the Divinity. As the Church teaches, "Everything in Christ's human nature is to be attributed to His Divine Person as its proper subject."[53] Thus the Christ re-presents the Godhead to us in flesh and blood, *"For in Him dwells all the fullness of Godhead bodily."* (Col. 2:9).

Another aspect of an icon is manifestation. The humanity of Christ is the icon that visibly manifests God in the created universe. In fact, St. John's Prologue, after declaring that *"The Word was made flesh, and dwelt among us"* (Jn. 1:14), goes on to announce, *"No one has at any time seen God. The only-begotten Son, who is in the bosom of the Father, He has revealed Him."* (Jn. 1:18). Jesus Christ, the Word Incarnate, reveals the invisible God to us in His sacred humanity. *"He who sees Me, sees Him who sent Me."* (Jn. 12:45). Hence, He is the visible, manifesting icon of the invisible God.

---

53 CCC #468.

An interesting corollary is the Franciscan view of the creation of man: *"Let Us make man to Our image and likeness"* (Gen. 1:26). According to the Franciscan thesis, when God creates He already foresees the Heart of Jesus—Christ is the 'first predestined' before the foundations of the world. He sees Jesus and He wills Him to be the perfect image and likeness of the invisible Godhead in the created universe by means of the Incarnation; then, beholding the excellence and perfection of Jesus Christ from all eternity, He creates the world. Christ is thus the Exemplar, the Model, the Alpha, the First. So God makes men according to His image and likeness *with Christ in mind*. Christ is the Prototype and we are modeled on Him. Consequently, when Adam falls and mars man's likeness to God, Christ repairs what was lost by His redemption so that we can indeed be conformed to Him. Is this not what Paul indicated in Romans? *"For those whom He has foreknown He has also predestined to become conformed to the image of the Son."* (Rom. 8:29). According to the Franciscan thesis, then, Jesus Christ is truly the *raison d'être* of all creation, of all that is not God.

This interpretation of Christ as the image of the invisible Godhead, foreknown before the creation of the universe, is found in the Church Fathers when they comment on the Wisdom passages of the Old Testament. For example they consistently interpret Proverbs 8:22-9:6 as referring to the Incarnate Word:

I [the Word made flesh] *was set up from eternity…when He prepared the heavens, I was present…when He balanced the foundations of the earth, I was with Him forming all things, and was delighted every day, playing before Him at all times; playing in the world. And My delights were to be with the children of men…*

That God had Incarnate Wisdom before Him when creating the universe according to this passage was held by St. Justin Martyr, St. Athanasius, St. Gregory of Nazianzen, St. Ambrose, St. John Chrysostom, St. Jerome, and many others as well.

Verse 15, firstborn of every creature

The next part of verse 15 reads that He is *"the firstborn of every creature."* (Col. 1:15). If, as we have maintained, the *Word made flesh* is the firstborn of every creature (as opposed to the Uncreated Word), then the Franciscan thesis is immensely enriched.

In support of this position, we recall the Hebrew notion of the 'firstborn' (cf. Ex. 13:2, 12-13). Of the flock, the firstborn male was to be redeemed or sacrificed; of the family, the firstborn son was to be redeemed. This Hebrew notion of the firstborn would not make sense if Paul were referring to the Divine, Uncreated Word as such. Moreover, the firstborn of a flock of sheep was itself a sheep; the firstborn male in the human family was a man like his brothers. In other words, the expression *"firstborn of every creature"* presumes that He Himself has a created nature just as *"firstborn among many brethren"* (Rom. 8:29) presumes that He has a human nature.

Finally, if the reference were to the Divine Person of the Word as Uncreated and Eternal quite apart from the Incarnation, then why the specific reference to the second Divine Person as opposed to the Father or the Holy Spirit? Why would there be a specific reference to the Uncreated Word instead of the Godhead? As we have noted, it is more consistent in this passage to see the subject of this Canticle as the Incarnate Word; it is inconsistent and even illogical to say that Paul suddenly changes the subject from Christ to the Uncreated Word.

This being the case, it is Jesus Christ who is *"the firstborn of every creature."* In the purpose of God's will, Christ has primacy over everything created. By this metaphor of the 'firstborn' the Apostle shows all creation as a family with Jesus Christ as the firstborn in the family of God's creation. He shares their nature by assuming the created, human nature from the Blessed Virgin Mary—firstborn of *every creature.* Chronologically, as we know, our Divine Lord is not the first creature born into the world; but in the plan of God, He is. Once again, what is first or 'firstborn' in the intention is last in execution, as we have frequently noted. Christ's primacy is, therefore, a primacy of excellence and priority in the intentions of God.

Priority in God

We recall here what the Subtle Doctor wrote:

> It can be said, therefore, that with the priority of nature God chose for His heavenly court all the angels and men He wished to have with their various degrees of perfection before He foresaw either sin or punishment.[54]

Christ in His sacred humanity has the highest degree of perfection in the heavenly court and is the first one predestined by God.

Scotus speaks of *ordo in praevisione divina*—that is, order or priority in the divine foresight and this precisely because God wills in a most orderly fashion.[55] For Scotus, as for the entire Franciscan school and for so many Fathers of the Church, order exists first within God among the Divine Persons, and then outside God via "orderly willing" and this is the foundation of intelligibility. Scotus writes,

> Therefore, God first loves Himself, and nearest in relation to this is His love for the soul of Christ that is to have the greatest glory in the world. And among all created things to be willed, this was first willed—an

---

54 BL. JOHN DUNS SCOTUS, *Ordinatio*, III, d. 7, q. 3.

55 Cf. BL. JOHN DUNS SCOTUS, *Opus Parisiense*, Lib III, d. 7, q. 4.

existence foreseen prior to all merit and hence prior to all demerit.[56]

He lists the priorities of intention in God with some minor variations in the *Ordinatio* and *Opus Parisiense*; but in the end they are all essentially the same: God is God and He first knows, loves, wills Himself; secondly, He wills to share His goodness in creation; thirdly, He wills "to be loved by Him who can love Him with the greatest love—speaking of the love of someone who is extrinsic to Himself. And *fourthly*, He foresees the union of that nature that must love Him with the greatest love even if no one had fallen."[57] From here God predestines His Immaculate Mother, then men and angels; then He foresees the fall and its remedy. It goes without saying that this priority in the divine intentions is outside of time. God is utterly simple and He does not will by a succession of time, but all at once. In one deliberation He wills creation with all of its order and beauty.

The thomistic thesis would see the priority in a different manner: first God knows or loves Himself; then He wills to create angels, then man, then the inferior creatures; He foresees the sin of Adam and wills Christ as Redeemer. In the thomistic outlook God wills first the less perfect (angels, men, other creatures), then He wills

---

56 BL. JOHN DUNS SCOTUS, *Reportatio Barcinonensis*, II, d. 7, q. 3.

57 BL. JOHN DUNS SCOTUS, *Opus Parisiense*, Lib III, d. 7, q. 4.

the most perfect (Jesus Christ). Moreover, Jesus Christ is willed, not only for the good of a fraction of the lesser perfect creatures (mankind only), but specifically as a remedy to mankind's sin. In this scheme, God does not will Christ for His own sake, nor as the final end of angels, but only as the final end for man on account of sin. To the thomists, Christ is not the first predestined and His primacy is relative to Adam's sin. Without redemption, Christ would not have come and He would not be the final end for man. Therefore, angels and men are willed independently of the prevision of sin; but Christ is not? Angels and men are predestined absolutely; but Christ relatively? Angels and men are foreseen before sin; but Christ is occasioned by sin?[58]

Scotus writes at length in response to this rationale:

If man had not sinned, there would have been no need for our redemption. But that God predestined this soul [of Christ] to so great a glory does not seem to be only on account of that [redemption], since the redemption or the glory of the soul to be redeemed is not comparable to the glory of Christ's soul. Neither is it likely that the highest good in creation is something that was merely occasioned only because of some lesser good; nor is it likely that He predestined Adam to such good before He predestined Christ; and yet this would follow [were the Incarnation occasioned by Adam's sin]. In fact, if the predestination of Christ's soul was

---

58 Cf. St. Thomas Aquinas, *Summa theol. III*, q. 1, a. 3.

for the sole purpose of redeeming others, something even more absurd would follow, namely, that in predestining Adam to glory, He would have foreseen Him as having fallen into sin before He predestined Christ to glory.[59]

Verses 16-17, Christian metaphysics

St. Paul's Canticle continues this revelation of the absolute primacy of Christ in the following verses.

> *For in Him were created all things in the heavens and on the earth, things visible and invisible, whether Thrones, or Dominations, or Principalities, or Powers. All things have been created through and unto Him, and He is before all creatures, and in Him all things hold together.* (Col. 1:16-17).

In these two verses Paul is talking about 'being'—metaphysics, plain and simple. But if the Apostle, as we have maintained, is consistently referring to Christ, and not the Uncreated Word, then all creatures are created

---

59 Bl. John Duns Scotus, *Ordinatio*, III, d. 7, q. 3.

in Christ, through Christ, and unto Christ.[60] Thus St. Bonaventure states that Christ is our metaphysics.[61]

1. In Christ—exemplary cause of creatures

To say that *"in Him were created all things"* means that Jesus Christ is the exemplary cause of all creatures. Since He is the Model, all creation is accomplished in Him, that is, all the perfections of creation reside in Christ as their Prototype. Jesus Christ, therefore, possesses in His sacred humanity all the perfections of the created universe, for in Him, *"are hidden all the treasures of wisdom and knowledge."* (Col. 2:3). God foresees the Incarnation and then wills all creation to reflect in various ways the perfections He sees in the most Sacred Heart. It could be no other way, for in decreeing the Incarnation God willed that Christ's human nature be divinized in the most perfect way possible—by personal union with the second Divine Person of the Most Holy Trinity. Nothing could be more exalted than the Heart of the God-Man; hence,

---

60 Cf. FR. DOMINIC UNGER, OFM CAP., *Franciscan Christology: Absolute and Universal Primacy of Christ*, in FS vol. 22 (N.S. 2) no. 4 (1942) 441-453; cf. also FR. MEILACH, *The Primacy of Christ in Doctrine and Life*, (Franciscan Herald Press, Chicago, 1964) 49-53; and cf. the exhaustive and masterful work on this subject FR. RUGGERO ROSINI, OFM, *Il Cristo nella Bibbia, nei Santi Padri, nel Vaticano II* (Editrice "Esca", Vicenza, 1980).

61 ST. BONAVENTURE, *Collationes in Hexaemeron*, col. 1, n. 17: "[Verbum] est medium metaphysicum reducens, et haec est tota nostra metaphysica."

all other created things of lesser perfection are created in Christ, their supreme Model.

2. Through Christ—secondary efficient cause of creatures

Obviously the Divinity is the efficient cause of all things outside of Itself; but, after the Godhead, St. Paul sees all things as created through Christ. Thus Jesus Christ is the secondary efficient cause of the universe. Since the sacred humanity of Christ does not pre-exist the universe, He does not produce the universe physically or even instrumentally. The Godhead creates the universe out of nothing and is alone the primary efficient cause. But God who, after knowing and loving Himself, wills Christ, foresees the infinite merits of the most Sacred Heart. From all eternity He foresees the perfect love of Jesus responding to His divine, creative love. Therefore, through Christ all things are created in this sense—Christ is the meritorious cause of all created things. The creation of Our Lady, the angels, the saints is accomplished in view of the merits of the Sacred Heart of Jesus. Thus, St. Paul: "*All things have been created through...Him.*"

3. Unto Christ—secondary final cause of all creatures

If *"all things have been created...unto Him"* as the Apostle states, then He is the final cause of all creation. The final cause indicates the goal which God has in mind. The goal of all creation is the glory of God—this is the ultimate final cause. Therefore, Jesus Christ as the *"one mediator between God and men"* (1 Tim. 2:5) is the secondary final cause that brings us to that ultimate goal through His Incarnation. Hence, we are created for Him, that is, He is our end. Only in union with Jesus can we glorify God and be glorified by Him. He is *"the way, the truth, and the life"* (Jn. 14:6) for whom we are created; and apart from Him we can do nothing (cf. Jn. 15:4-5). In other words, God has directed the entire universe towards Himself (final cause) through Christ (intermediate or secondary final cause).

After these lessons in metaphysics, the Apostle adds that *"He is before all creatures."* He is not speaking of the Incarnate Word in terms of the chronology of execution, but in terms of the eternal intentions of God. In the mind of God Christ is the first creature—the Alpha (cf. Apoc. 22:13).

"And in Him all things hold together"—that is, Christ sustains us in being. Apart from Him we do not exist; but rather, we exist by Him.

Verse 18, headship and primacy

"Again, He is the head of His body, the Church; He, who is the beginning, the firstborn from the dead, that in all things He may have the first place [primatum tenens].*"* (Col. 1:18).

Jesus Christ is the Head of the Mystical Body, the Church. What is the Church—redeemed humanity only? Or all angels and men predestined to grace and glory before the foundation of the world? St. Paul speaks of the Incarnate Word as *"the head of every Principality and Power."* (Col. 2:10).

Thus Scotus is on solid ground when he speaks of the Church as a single heavenly court. "With a priority of nature God chose for His heavenly court all the angels and men He wished to have with their various degrees of perfection."[62] And who is the Head of this celestial family? Scotus writes, "Since the positive act of the divine will regarding the predestined in common precedes all the acts of His will concerning either the reprobate or the fall of anyone whatever, it does not seem that the predestination of Christ to be the Head of the heavenly court, was occasioned by the fall or by the demerit of the reprobate."[63]

---

[62] BL. JOHN DUNS SCOTUS, *Ordinatio*, III, d. 7, q. 3.

[63] BL. JOHN DUNS SCOTUS, *Reportatio Barcinonensis*, II, d. 7, q. 3.

If, as Scotus maintains, Christ is predestined as the Head of the entire celestial court, then He is predestined absolutely. If He is the *"firstborn of every creature"* He has an absolute primacy. Or if *"in Him were created all things in the heavens and on the earth, things visible and things invisible, whether Thrones, or Dominations, or Principalities, or Powers"* (Col. 1:16), then He is predestined above all angels and saints and this quite apart from any consideration of sin. Or if *"all things have been created through and unto Him and He is before all creatures"* (Col. 1:16), then He is the first of the predestined since angels or men cannot be predestined in Him if He is not already foreseen. Christ is, then, the Head over all creation, all the elect, all the Church—angels and men alike—*"that in all things He may have the first place"* (Col. 1:18). To say that Jesus Christ is Head only of fallen mankind and not of angels, is to deny that He has primacy *"in all things"* as a result of His headship over the Church.

The Franciscan thesis maintains that there is only one economy of divine grace which is mediated through Jesus Christ, as opposed to the thomists who maintain that angels and Adam and Eve belong to the original economy of grace but, after the fall of Adam and Eve, God willed a second and better economy of grace for fallen mankind. If that were the case, then why should the angels pay homage to the Word *made flesh*? Yet the Apostle clearly says,

At the name of Jesus every knee should bend of those in heaven, on earth, and under the earth and every tongue should confess that the Lord Jesus Christ is in the glory of God the Father." (Phil. 2:10-11).

St. Paul, as we noted earlier, holds that God's eternal decree (*"His good pleasure"* or *"His purpose"*) was *"to sum up all things under the headship of Christ, both in the heavens and those on the earth"* (Eph. 1:10).[64] This is why the Apostle can maintain that the Incarnate Word is set *"above every Principality and Power and Virtue and Domination—in short, above every name that is named, not only in this world, but also in that which is to come. And all things He made subject under His feet, and Him He gave as head over all the Church, which indeed is His body, the completion of Him who fills all with all."* (Eph. 1:21-23; cf. Heb. 1).

The point to be emphasized here is that if the Word made flesh is predestined as Head of the angels who are part of the Church, then clearly He is predestined first and absolutely before any foreseen fall of Adam and has absolute primacy over all creation. If, on the other hand, angels were not part of the Church nor under the headship of Christ, then the Apostle would make no sense when he writes,

Yes, to me, the very least of all saints, there was given this grace, to announce among the Gentiles the good tidings

---

64 Cf. the argument for this translation in Section V, A, v. 10

> *of the unfathomable riches of Christ, and to enlighten all*
> *men as to what is the dispensation of the mystery which*
> *was hidden from eternity in God, who created all things:*
> *in order that through the Church there be made known*
> *to the Principalities and the Powers in the heavens the*
> *manifold wisdom of God according to the eternal purpose*
> *which He accomplished in Christ Jesus our Lord.* (Eph.
> 3:8-11).

This would be an odd statement, *"that through the Church there be made known to the Principalities and the Powers in the heavens the manifold wisdom of God,"* unless the angels are under the headship of Christ as part of the Church.

Long before Scotus and the Franciscan Order, St. Anastasius of Sinai, a seventh century Church Father, wrote of the eternal predestination of Christ and His Church as follows:

> All creation, visible and invisible, was first
> constructed and prefigured, according to her image
> [the Church] and that of Christ her spouse. For this
> is the mystery which God first predestined before the
> ages and generations…Now, when the Apostle of God
> said, *'all things, both visible and invisible, were created*
> *in Christ,'* he plainly shows and teaches that even the

invisible creature was prefigured and made in Christ and the Church.[65]

In recent times, an expert on angelology and demonology, the chief exorcist of the Diocese of Rome, Fr. Gabriel Amorth, wrote a most concise and lucid summation of the Franciscan thesis in his book *An Exorcist Tells his Story*. Before he 'tells his story', he begins by "first stating some basic facts about God's plan for creation." He writes:

> All too often we have the wrong concept of creation, and we take for granted the following wrong sequence of events. We believe that one day God created the angels; that He put them to the test, although we are not sure which test; and that as a result we have the division among angels and demons. The angels were rewarded with heaven, and the demons were punished with hell. Then we believe that on another day God created the universe, the minerals, the plants, the animals, and, in the end, man. In the Garden of Eden, Adam and Eve obeyed Satan and disobeyed God; thus they sinned. At this point, to save mankind, God decided to send His Son.

> This is not what the Bible teaches us, and it is not the teaching of the Fathers. If this were so, the angels

---

[65] ST. ANASTASIUS OF SINAI, In *Hexaëm. praef.*; PG 89, 854; Cf. FR. DOMINIC UNGER, OFM CAP., *Christ, the Exemplar and Final Scope of All Creation according to Anastasius of Sinai*, in FS vol. 9, no. 2 (1949) 156-164.

and creation would remain strangers to the mystery of Christ. If we read the Prologue of the Gospel of John and the two Christological hymns that open the letters to the Ephesians and the Colossians, we see that Christ is *'the firstborn of all creatures'* (Col. 1:15). Everything was created for Him and in the expectation of Him. There is no theological discussion that makes any sense if it asks whether Christ would have been born without the sin of Adam. Christ is the center of creation; all creatures, both heavenly (the angels) and earthly (man) find in Him their summation. On the other hand, we can affirm that, given the sin of our forebears, Christ's coming assumed a particular role: He came as Savior. The core of His action is contained within the Paschal Mystery: through the blood of His Cross, He reconciles all things in the heavens (angels) and on earth (man) to God. The role of every creature is dependent on this christocentric understanding.[66]

Verses 19-20, the test of the angels: the Incarnation

It is noteworthy that the Greek word *apokatallaxai*, translated as *"reconciled,"* actually means 'leading to unity in the same goal'. Thus verses 19-20 might be translated more accurately into English as follows: *"For it has pleased God the Father that in Him all His fullness should dwell, and that He* should lead all things to unity in Christ,

---

66 FR. GABRIEL AMORTH, *An Exorcist Tells his Story* (Ignatius Press, San Francisco, 1999) 19-20.

whether on the earth or in the heavens, making peace through the blood of His Cross." (Col. 1:19-20). Thus God willed it before He began creating out of nothing—that all things be unified and centered in Jesus. It comes as no surprise, then, that the Franciscan school affirms that the test of the angels was centered on the mystery of the Incarnation. Shown a vision of the Virgin with the Divine Child, those angels who accepted Jesus and Mary as their King and Queen are the blessed angels and those who refused the reign of the Sacred Hearts of Jesus and Mary are the cursed demons who say, *"non serviam"*—"I will not serve."

Thus the evil one in Genesis 3 goes after the first woman, Eve, because he had been shown a vision of the Woman with Child and was immediately searching for her—"Is this the predestined Virgin? Let us tempt her! Let us ruin God's plan and make ourself the center of creation! Let us entice her to *'be as gods'* (Gen. 3:5) apart from Christ!" The serpent allured her and she disobeyed God's plan which was that we might receive of the *"fullness of the Godhead"* (cf. Eph. 3:19; Col. 2:8-10; Jn. 1:16) and become *"partakers of the divine nature"* (2 Pt. 1:4) and *"sons of God"* (cf. Jn. 1:12-13) through the Incarnation.

Interestingly, when Jesus Christ walks this earth the demons recognize Him. *"I know who Thou art, the Holy One of God,"* says one demon (Mk. 1:24). Another *"legion"* of demons cry out from two possessed men in the country of the Gerasenes, *"What have we to do with Thee, Son of God? Hast Thou come here to torment us before the time?"* (Mt. 8:29). And the demons fear that He has come to destroy them (cf. Mk. 1:24; Lk. 5:34). Their recognition of the Incarnate Word and their fear of torment and destruction in His presence indicate that they have foreknowledge of Him and that their damnation and torture is to be subject to the God-Man and His Immaculate Mother whom they eternally rejected before the visible world was even created.

Recapitulation of Bl. Scotus and the Scriptures

In studying and meditating on the Pauline texts of Ephesians 1:3-10, Romans 8:29 and Colossians 1:15-20 in conjunction with the insights of Bl. John Duns Scotus, a clear picture has been brought into focus. Jesus Christ is at the heart of God's creative plan before creation is even set in motion. This absolute predestination of Christ to the maximum grace and glory manifests a fixed plan in the intention of God the Creator. Christ is foreordained in the divine plan as King of all creation and Head of all the elect, angels and saints alike. Consequently, Jesus Christ has primacy over all creatures, over all that is not God. His is a primacy that is not contingent upon or relative to any created thing whatsoever; rather, the primacy of Christ is absolute and not occasioned by man's need for redemption or divinization.

The Incarnation is the greatest work of God in all the created universe. No other created nature, however graced and glorified, is united to God in the oneness of Person. Only Christ, by virtue of the hypostatic union, is elevated to this place of absolute primacy. As such, He is the creature most perfectly glorified by the Most Holy Trinity. This was God's eternal decree. God freely willed to communicate His love, His goodness, and indeed His very divinity in its fullness to the created nature of the Word made flesh.

Moreover, the Incarnate Word is the perfect Glorifier of God in all creation. In His human nature He gives more glory to the Triune God than all the angels and saints put together. Thus Jesus Christ, the greatest work of God *ad extra*, is willed for His own sake (to be united to the Divinity in the Person of the Word) and for the glory of God (to be the perfect Glorifier of the Trinity in creation).

This is realized in the fullness of time because what is first in the intention of the Divine Architect, namely the Incarnation, comes last in the execution of His plan. Thus the mystery, hidden from men in times past, has now been fully unveiled to us in Jesus Christ. In Him we see the eternal purpose of God. In Him all things unfold according to the good pleasure of God.

Therefore, all creation finds its reason for existence in Him. God foresees Christ from all eternity and creates all things based on what He sees in Christ. Jesus is the Model, the Exemplar, the Prototype of all creation. All the goodness in creation is but a reflection of the perfection God saw from all eternity in the God-Man.

All creation exists through the Word Incarnate. God alone is the efficient cause of all creation; but, after knowing and loving Himself, He wills Christ to be the intermediate cause of all being. He foresees the infinite merits of the most Sacred Heart of Jesus and thus through Christ all things are created in the sense that Christ is the meritorious cause of all created things. God sees the infinite merits of the God-Man and this is the secondary efficient cause of all created things.

All creatures exist for Christ as their final cause. The goal of all creation is the glory of God—this is the ultimate end of angels and men. Only in union with the God-Man are we able to glorify God and be glorified by Him. In other words, God has ordained that the elect reach their ultimate goal through the Incarnation.

It is this divine decree which orders all things. While God wills all creation at once, there is an order and priority in His intention before He even begins the execution of His plan. God wills in a most orderly fashion. After knowing, loving and willing Himself from all eternity, He freely, gratuitously wills to share His Divine Essence with a creature extrinsic to Himself. Thus the first predestined, the one closest to Himself in the created universe, is the Christ whose created nature is to be united to the Godhead in the personal union with the Word. In this same decree, God wills that Jesus be born of a woman; thus blessed Mary is jointly predestined with Him to be His Immaculate Virgin Mother. Simultaneously, the angels are predestined to grace and glory in Christ, Head of the heavenly court, and the saints, before any consideration of sin, are predestined to grace and glory as God's adopted children in Christ Jesus. This is God's eternal plan.

Foreseeing the fall of Adam and Eve, God wills that Jesus and Mary repair original sin by the work of Redemption as the Redeemer and Coredemptrix of the human race. This redemption is not the primary reason for the Incarnation, but rather a secondary motive which, while it does not occasion God's greatest work in the created universe, nonetheless, manifests His supreme love and mercy to a sinful race and remedies a most dire need for mankind if they are to profit from the blessings offered in the Incarnation.

The absolute primacy of Jesus Christ underscores the centrality of Christ in the whole created universe. Creation is fundamentally christocentric. This means that all rational, free creatures find their reason for existence in Him alone; either they live for Him or die without Him, and this forever—Heaven or Hell. In a word, all the elect, angels and saints, are predestined in Him before the foundations of the world as members of His Mystical Body, the Church. Christ is the Head; we are His members.

We conclude this section of the Scriptural foundations of the absolute predestination and primacy of Christ with a reflection on the implications of Ephesians 2:20.

D. Eph. 2:20 Christ the chief cornerstone

The day after His triumphal entry into Jerusalem and His cleansing of the temple, Jesus spoke to the chief priests and elders saying, *"Did you never read in the Scriptures, 'The stone which the builders rejected has become the cornerstone; by the Lord has this been done, and it is wonderful in our eyes?'"* (Mt. 21:42). In willing the Incarnation, God has indeed done what is wonderful in our eyes. He is the Divine Architect of the universe who, in His immense love and goodness, freely chose to communicate Himself *ad extra* to a created nature in a most perfect way: union with Him in the Person of the Word. From all eternity God foreordained the Incarnation and willed that Jesus Christ be *"the chief cornerstone."* (Eph. 2:20).

This is God's eternal decree: His plan is to build a Temple and fill it with His glory. He wills this in a most orderly manner so that the entire universe and its history unfold *"according to His good pleasure"* (Eph. 1:9) with a fixed purpose in mind.

First, God knows and loves Himself. Then, He loves that which is nearest to Himself, namely the sacred humanity of Jesus—He predestines Christ to the greatest possible glory by way of the hypostatic union and He foreordains that Christ be the secure foundation of His

Temple;[67] in that same decree He also predestines Mary Immaculate to the maximum grace and glory (after Christ) by way of virginal and divine maternity. Then, God loves angels and men by predestining them to be part of His Temple in, through, and unto Christ Jesus, their chief cornerstone. *"In Him the whole structure is closely fitted together and grows into a temple holy in the Lord"* (Eph. 2:21).

To the Jewish people there was a keen sense that the temple was a microcosm of the entire universe.[68] Indeed the temple of Jerusalem was made according to a meticulous, divine pattern (cf. Ex. 25-28; Heb. 8:5). Yet, even in all its splendor, this temple was still a *"mere copy"* of the true Temple (Heb. 9:24).

Where is the true Temple to be found? Where is this Exemplary Cause containing in itself all the perfections of the created universe? Hear the voice of the Father and watch His Glory descend and fill His Temple:

> *And behold, the heavens were opened…, and he* [John the Baptist] *saw the Spirit of God descending as a dove and coming upon Him. And behold, a voice from the*

---

67 Cf. Fr. Dominic Unger, OFM Cap., *Christ Jesus the Secure Foundation: According to St. Cyril of Alexandria*, in FS vol. 7, no. 1, 3, 4 (1947).

68 Cf. Flavius Josephus, *The Antiquities of the Jews*, Book 3, c. 7, 179-180, reported in *The Works of Josephus*, trans. by William Whiston (Hendrickson Publishers, Peabody, 1988) 90; cf. also *The Wars of the Jews*, Book 5, c. 11, 458-459 (also in *The Works of Josephus*).

heavens said, 'This is My beloved Son, in whom I am well pleased' (Mt. 3:16-17).

Jesus Christ is the Temple foreseen before the ages and predestined to give perfect glory to the Triune God: *"I have glorified Thee on earth; I have accomplished the work that Thou hast given Me to do."* (Jn. 17:4). Jesus Christ is furthermore filled most perfectly with God's glory: *"And now do Thou, Father, glorify Me with Thyself, with the glory that I had with Thee before the world existed"* (Jn. 17:5).

While Jesus is God's true and perfect Temple in and of Himself, nonetheless, God has made Him the *chief cornerstone* of the Temple which is His Body, the Church (cf. Jn. 2:19-21; Col. 1:18; Eph. 1:22-23). Christ is the first one predestined, the main cornerstone of the foundation. God sees Him first in His intention: *"For in Him were created all things in the heavens and on the earth, things visible and things invisible"* (Col. 1:16). Then He wills to create and order all things *"through and unto Him"* so that all is built upon Jesus as the chief cornerstone—"*In Him the whole structure is closely fitted together and grows into a temple holy in the Lord, in Him you too are being built together into a dwelling place for God in the Spirit"* (Eph. 2:21-22; cf. 2 Cor. 6:16).

Thus angels and men are predestined to grace and glory in Him: *"And the glory that Thou hast given Me, I have given to them, that they may be one, even as We are one"* (Jn. 17:22). In Christ we are to glorify God and to be filled with God's glory. God orders everything to this end. And so St. Paul writes of *"building up the body of Christ, until we all attain to the unity of the faith and of the deep knowledge of the Son of God, to perfect manhood, to the mature measure of the fullness of Christ...and so grow up in Him who is the head, Christ. For from Him the whole body...derives its increase to the building up of itself in love"* (Eph. 4:11-16; cf. Rom. 8:28). The more we mature to our full stature in Christ, the more perfectly we will glorify God and be filled with His glory.

This is God's eternal plan—that Jesus Christ be the King of all creation and Lord of all the universe. We speak of an absolute primacy willed by God for its own sake; a primacy not occasioned by a lesser good nor an evil act committed by a creature. He alone is *"the Alpha and the Omega, the beginning and the end."* (Apoc. 21:6). As *"the Blessed and only Sovereign, the King of kings and Lord of lords"* (1 Tim. 6:15; cf. Apoc. 17:14; 19:16), Jesus Christ is subject to no one save His Father in Heaven. And since the divine plan has now been realized in the *"fullness of time"* (Gal. 4:4) and since the mystery of Christ has now been proclaimed throughout the world (cf. Col. 1:25-2:3), we are duty bound to:

Draw near to Him, a living stone, rejected indeed by men but chosen and honored by God. Be you yourselves living stones, built thereon into a spiritual house, a holy priesthood, to offer up spiritual sacrifices acceptable to God through Jesus Christ. Hence Scripture says, 'Behold, I lay in Sion a chief cornerstone, chosen, precious; and he who believes in it shall not be put to shame.' (1 Pt. 2:4-5).

Ave Maria!

Chapter 6

Mediation of grace and glory

Having established the headship of Christ over all the elect, both men and angels, and His absolute primacy in all creation, we can now unveil the beauty of God's plan in relation to us men in particular. When we realize that Christ was the first predestined to grace and glory, and that the elect were predestined to grace and glory in Him, it becomes apparent that Christ came as our Mediator, sin or no sin. God's eternal plan was that our entire spiritual life be centered upon the mediation of the God-Man.

Two types of mediation

According to Scotus, Christ mediates in two ways: *ex unione* and *ex gratia.*

Christ's very existence as the God-Man mediates between God and men *ex unione,* namely because of His union with the Word. He is the Son of God made man, "the Head of the heavenly court,"[69] the Church. It is in this strict sense of mediation as Head by virtue

---

[69] Bl. John Duns Scotus, *Reportatio Barcinonensis*, II, d. 7, q. 3.

of the hypostatic union that *"there is one God, and one Mediator between God and men, Himself a man, Christ Jesus"* (1 Tim. 2:5; cf. Heb. 8:6). Because Christ's sacred humanity alone is personally united to the Word, no other creature can share in this unique mediation of Christ *ex unione* as Head. Scotus points out that "there could never be but one Head in the Church from which there is derived the influx of graces upon the members."[70] So Jesus is the Head (Col. 1:18); in Him dwells the fullness of Divinity corporally (2:9); from Him, as the Head, the whole body is supplied and built up (2:19).

But He is also the Mediator of grace to the elect *ex gratia*, that is, from the fullness of grace He possesses as the Son of Man. St. John tells us that the Incarnate Word was *"full of grace...And of His fullness we have all received, grace upon grace"* (Jn. 1:14,16). Unlike His mediation *ex unione* as Head, His mediation *ex gratia* is shared by other creatures in varying degrees. Here His mediation flows from the plenitude of grace He possesses as true man. In this sense Jesus is the fountain of graces from which all graces flow to the elect.

Christ's mediation elevates

The principal blessing that men receive from Christ as Mediator is their elevation to grace and glory. By humbling Himself to partake of our created nature He

---

70 BL. JOHN DUNS SCOTUS, *Ordinatio*, III, d. 13, q. 4, n. 8.

makes us *"partakers of the divine nature"* (2 Pt. 1:4); in the first place He saves us from our metaphysical deficiency by elevating us from mere natural creatures to the sublime heights of supernatural creatures. The grace of man's elevation comes through the Incarnation:

> *For you know the graciousness of our Lord Jesus Christ— how, being rich* [divine], *He became poor* [human] *for your sakes, that by His poverty* [humanity] *you might become rich* [divine] (2 Cor. 8:9).

Through faith and Baptism we are justified, raised to the dignity of the children of God: *"But to as many as received Him He gave the power of becoming sons of God; to those who believe in His name"* (Jn. 1:12; cf. Jn. 3:5).

Redemption presupposes mediation

Given the fact of the eternal and absolute predestination of Christ and the predestination of the elect in Him, Christ's mediation is invaluable quite apart from any consideration of Adam's fall. In fact, sin can only be understood as a sequel to grace. So sin or no sin, Christ is predestined to be Mediator of grace and glory to both men and angels. After the fall, He works out our redemption by His sacrifice on the Cross. Jesus Christ *becomes* the Redeemer because He *is* the Mediator; not vice versa. While His work of mediation has value and meaning in its own right, His work of redemption, on the other hand, presupposes

His coming as Mediator through the Incarnation. Note well that redemption necessarily depends upon the Word becoming flesh—if Jesus did not come in the flesh there would be no possibility of His redeeming us. However, the Word becoming flesh does not depend upon the redemption, or anything else for that matter. Jesus comes as the Mediator of grace and glory; because of sin we speak of the *redemptive* Incarnation.

Fr. Dominic Unger writes:

Christ is the First-born and the Head of all the elect. That is the unmistakable doctrine of St. Paul (cf. Rom. 8:29; Col. 1:15; Eph. 1:3-6; and also Prov. 8:22). But that predestination in which Christ is First-born and the Head, is the original predestination of all men: according to St. Paul there is only one predestination; not two—one at the creation without Christ, and one after the fall with Christ. There was only one plan of divine adoption and that was before the foundation of the world and in Christ Jesus. God wanted to elevate men to grace and glory; but He never willed to do that except through Christ. So Christ was in the very first picture of predestination and there is no longer rhyme or reason in speaking of His coming merely to redeem.[71]

Now included in that "very first picture of predestination"—united with Christ in God's plan

---

71 FR. DOMINIC UNGER, OFM CAP., *Franciscan Christology*, in FS vol. 23 (N.S. vol. 2) no. 4 (1942).

104

above all angels and men—was the Blessed Virgin Mary. Alongside the New Adam there was foreseen the New Eve—the Woman with her Offspring (cf. Gen. 3:15), the Virgin with Child (cf. Is. 7:14).

The place of Mary—joint predestination

The Franciscan thesis upholds that the Immaculate was predestined in Christ *par excellence,* chosen *"in Him before the foundation of the world...* [to] *be holy and without blemish in His sight in love"* (cf. Eph.1:4). She is chosen prior to all the other elect because she is jointly predestined with Christ as His Mother. The Venerable Fr. Gabriel Allegra writes:

> Since God the Father has chosen us in Christ before the creation of the world, it is simply logical that the first willed, the first loved, the first elected one of the Father is Jesus Christ. Now since Jesus Christ, the Incarnate Word and Lord of the universe and particularly of humanity, is Himself a man and, therefore, our Brother, He had to have a Mother. And, as Pope Pius IX appropriately said, by the same eternal decree in which God willed the Incarnation of His Only-begotten Son, He also willed specifically His Son's Immaculate Mother...

> What God has determined from all eternity before the creation of the world is fulfilled in time. And what is fulfilled is nothing else than the carrying

out of God's decree from the beginning, before He created the angelic spirits, the earth, and mankind. The action of God, like His Word, is an infallible and creative action.

In reference to the Immaculate Mother of the Incarnate Word, the Holy Trinity performed this miracle of miracles 2000 years ago. But this work, the creation of Mary, which together with the Incarnation of His Word is the first and 'greatest work of God' (Bl. John Duns Scotus) and coterminous with God's life, is hidden in the eternity of His eternal design.[72]

Exalted above all creatures

According to St. Francis of Assisi and the Franciscan school after him, the Holy Virgin was predestined to be the beloved Daughter of God the Father, the loving Mother of God the Son, the holy Spouse of the Holy Spirit—the one chosen, predestined and exalted by the Most Holy Trinity above all other creatures. St. Francis speaks of her exalted place in God's plan in his beautiful *Antiphon for the Office of the Passion*:

Holy Virgin Mary, *among women there is no one like you born in the world.* You are the Daughter and Servant of the Most High and Supreme King and Father of

---

[72] VEN. FR. GABRIEL ALLEGRA, OFM, *Mary's Immaculate Heart: A Way to God* (Franciscan Herald Press, Chicago, 1982) 19-20. He dedicates an entire chapter on Our Lady in relation to the Trinity; cf. p. I, c. 3.

Heaven; You are the Mother of our Most Holy Lord Jesus Christ; You are the Spouse of the Holy Spirit. Pray for us with St. Michael the Archangel and all the powers of the heavens and all the Saints to your most holy, beloved Son, our Lord and Master.[73]

In his *Salutation to the Blessed Virgin* the Seraphic Patriarch writes:

Hail, O Lady, Mary, holy Mother of God: You are the Virgin made Church, *chosen* by the most holy Father in Heaven, whom He consecrated with His most holy beloved Son and with the Holy Spirit, the Paraclete. *In you there was and is all the fullness of grace and every good...*[74]

St. Maximilian Mary Kolbe exclaims:

I adore You, O our heavenly Father, for having placed in the most pure womb of Mary Your only-

---

[73] St. Francis of Assisi, Antiphon for the Office of the Passion, in *Bibliotheca Franciscana Ascetica Medii Aevi, Tom. XII: Opusula Sancti Patris Francisci Assisiensis* (Grottaferrata, 1978) 193; cf. Francis of Assisi: *Early Documents I* (New City Press, New York, 1999) 141. Cf. Fr. Johannes Schneider's commentary in *Virgo Ecclesia Facta: The Presence of Mary in the Crucifix of San Damiano and in the Office of the Passion of St. Francis of Assisi*, (Academy of the Immaculate, New Bedford, 2004).

[74] St. Francis of Assisi, Salutation of the Blessed Virgin, in *Bibliotheca Franciscana Ascetica Medii Aevi, Tom. XII: Opusula Sancti Patris Francisci Assisiensis* (Grottaferrata, 1978) 299; cf. Francis of Assisi: *Early Documents I* (New City Press, New York, 1999) 163.

begotten Son; I adore You, O Son of God, because You condescended to enter her womb and became truly her actual Son; I adore You, O Holy Spirit, because You deigned to form in her immaculate womb the body of the Son of God; I adore You, O Most Holy Trinity, *for having ennobled the Immaculate in such a divine way.*[75]

In the same passage St. Maximilian speaks to the Immaculate saying:

Allow others to surpass me in zeal for your exaltation, and me to surpass them, so that by means of such noble rivalry your glory may increase ever more profoundly, ever more rapidly, ever more intensely as *He* who *has exalted you so indescribably above all other beings* Himself desires...*For you God has created the world.* For you God has called even me into existence.[76]

The Franciscan school, then, is a harmonious chorus singing of how God foreordained the Immaculate, before any consideration of sin, to be *"clothed with the sun, and the moon under her feet, and upon her head a crown of twelve stars"* (Apoc. 12:1). Without sin, she would have been all this, but she would not have had to cry out *"in her travail and...the anguish of delivery"* (Apoc. 12:2)

75 St. Maximilian Mary Kolbe, *Scritti* (ENMI, Rome, 1997) 1305.

76 Ibid.

when bringing forth the body of Christ, the Church, by way of coredemption.

The place of Marian mediation

Since God, who wills in a most orderly fashion, placed the mediation of Jesus Christ (the God-Man) at the center of creation, it follows that immediately under Christ, the Head of the Church, He placed the Immaculate. She is the most exalted creature (after Christ) because of her Immaculate Conception. She is truly *"full of grace"* (Lk. 1:28) and all the graces of Christ the Head are found in her in their fullness as in no other human person. While no one, not even the Mother of God, can participate in Christ's mediation as Head *ex unione*; she does share in His mediation as the fountain of divine grace *ex gratia* and this in a unique fashion above all the elect. St. Bernard writes,

> God has placed in Mary the plenitude of every good, in order to have us understand that if there is any trace of hope in us, any trace of grace, any trace of salvation, it flows from her.[77]

The Virgin Mary as mere creature is under the headship of Christ as God-Man (Christ's mediation *ex unione*); but as Mother of God she stands with and

---

[77] St. Bernard of Clairvaux, *Hom. in nativitat.* BVM, n. 6, PL 183, 441.

subordinate to Christ who, as true man, is the fountain of all graces (Christ's mediation *ex gratia*). For this reason Our Lady is sometimes referred to as the 'neck' through which flow all the graces of Christ the Head to the members. From the divine perspective, then, the Creator wills to bestow grace and glory on the elect through Christ the Mediator and Mary the Mediatrix. All grace and glory for men and angels alike flows by irrevocable divine decree through the Sacred Hearts of Jesus and Mary.[78] God's well ordered plan, therefore, is that in the created realm He will bestow all good things upon Jesus Christ and, through, with and in Him, upon His Immaculate Virgin Mother. Through the Sacred Hearts we receive every grace, which in the first instance is an elevating and divinizing grace that makes us children of God (after the fall that grace becomes redemptive as well).

---

78 The Hearts of Jesus and Mary traditionally represent Their persons—all graces flow to us from God through the mediation of Jesus and Mary as represented by Their Sacred Hearts. Devotion to the Sacred Heart of Jesus is a devotion to the physical heart of Jesus, the God-Man, which is adorable (latria) by virtue of the hypostatic union; it is a devotion to that which is symbolized by the heart, namely, the interior, moral center of the person—hence, devotion to the burning love of Jesus towards God in His sacred humanity and His burning love for men in both His sacred humanity and divinity; ultimately, it is a devotion to the Person of the Word who has assumed our human nature. With regards to devotion to the Immaculate Heart of Mary, it is a devotion to the physical heart of the Immaculate Virgin Mother of God which is venerable (hyperdulia) by virtue of her Immaculate Conception and Divine Maternity; it is a devotion to her burning love for the Most Holy Trinity and for mankind; ultimately, it is a devotion to the most exalted person of Mary, created by God above all angels and men.

Action and reaction

"Action and reaction"[79]—this was St. Maximilian Mary Kolbe's way of summarizing Scotus' thought on mediation. God acts; He creates in an orderly manner. The creature "reacts" (responds) to His love and grace. We see this first and foremost in the human nature of Christ which, once created, burns with unspeakable love for the Most Holy Trinity—action and reaction. We see this again in the Blessed Virgin Mary who is, after Christ, the summit of God's creative action and who burns in all her created personhood with love for Jesus and for the entire Trinity—action and reaction. We also see this in the angels and the saints.

With regards to mediation, then, St. Bonaventure sums it up nicely when he writes that Our Lady "is Mediatrix between us and Christ, as Christ [is Mediator] between us and God."[80] As God acts through Them to bless the elect, so the elect must return through Them to God.

St. Maximilian explains the descent of divine grace to man (i.e. "action") in this way:

> The Immaculate Virgin is the most perfect among creatures, She has been elevated above every creature

---

79 Cf. St. Maximilian Kolbe, *Scritti* 1291.

80 St. Bonaventure, *Sent. III*, d. 3, pars 1, a. 1, q. 2: (Maria)... "Mediatrix est inter nos et Christum, sicut Christus inter nos et Deum."

and is a 'divine' creature in an ineffable manner. The Son of God, in fact, descended from the Father by means of the Spirit, He dwelt in Her, He became incarnate within Her and She became the Mother of God, Mother of the God-Man, Mother of Jesus. From that moment every grace—which comes forth from the Father through Jesus, the Incarnate Son, and the Spirit who dwells in the Immaculate—is distributed precisely through the Immaculate.[81]

God's action towards us, then, is to bestow grace upon grace through Jesus and Mary, a reality that is visualized in devotion to the Sacred Heart of Jesus and Immaculate Heart of Mary. Our "reaction" must be a love ascending along the same path by which His love descended to us. Stated concisely, man's return to God his ultimate end occurs through the mediation of Jesus Christ and the Blessed Virgin Mary. Thus St. Maximilian writes,

Every man's end is to belong to God through Jesus, the Mediator before the Father, and to belong to Jesus through the Mediatrix of all graces, the Immaculate.[82]

---

81 ST. MAXIMILIAN KOLBE, *Scritti* 1224.

82 Ibid. 1329.

The Sacred Hearts

Tying this into our theme, this means that Jesus and Mary were predestined absolutely to the maximum grace and glory and that all the elect were predestined to grace and glory in and through Them. Sin or no sin, God's design is that all graces come to men and angels through the Hearts of Jesus and Mary and that they return to Him by these most Sacred Hearts. Mediation of grace and glory through the Incarnate Word and His Immaculate Mother is at the heart of God's creative plan; the elect are predestined *"before the foundation of the world"* (Eph. 1:4) in Jesus and Mary. We might illustrate God's perfect plan for our salvation and sanctification as follows: [*please turn the page*]

Absolute Predestination

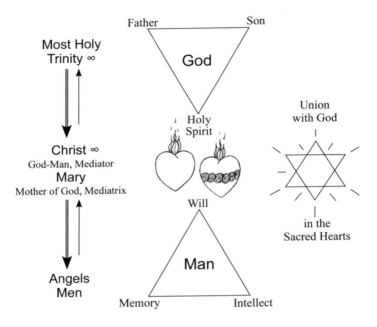

(Eternal decree not occasioned by sin)

All the positive blessings of the Incarnation are realized in this way. Jesus and Mary are predestined absolutely and placed at the center of God's creative purpose. Thus, through Their Sacred Hearts man is elevated to a participation in the divine nature (2 Pt. 1:4; 2 Cor. 8:9); he is transformed into a child of God (Jn. 1:12; Rom. 8:14-17; Eph. 1:5); he is predestined *"before the foundation of the world"* to be *"holy and without blemish in His sight in love"* (Eph. 1:4); he is shown the truth about God (Jn. 1:18; 12:45; Mt. 11:27; Heb. 1:1-2; etc.).

The Divine Mercy

This is God's plan from the beginning and it is immutable. However, because of Adam and Eve's sin we find ourselves in an insurmountable predicament. A barrier has been placed between us and God through our sin in Adam. Thus through original sin man chose to disobey God's designs of mediation and a barrier was set up that we finite creatures could not break through. God extends mercy and wills that the Mediator and Mediatrix of all graces shatter the barrier that thwarts His plan in our regard. Jesus and Mary become the Redeemer and Coredemptrix of the human race; Their Hearts are pierced through and redeeming love gushes forth for the whole world. Although the Incarnation would not have been redemptive (*quoad modum*) if Adam had not sinned; nonetheless, the fixed plan of God remains entirely intact (*quoad substantiam*)—all graces come to men and angels from God through the mediation of Jesus and Mary; only now the Mediator and Mediatrix are also Redeemer and Coredemptrix of the human race.

Absolute Predestination

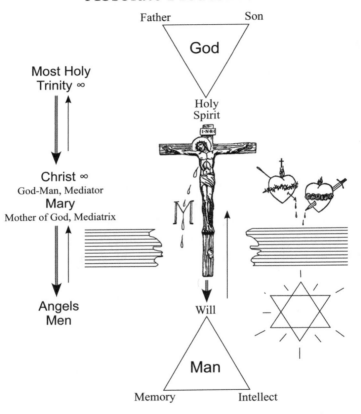

(Same eternal decree, but the redemptive mode of
the Incarnation is occasioned by sin)

The purpose of God is not altered in its substance—Christ and Mary are predestined to the maximum grace and glory; the elect are predestined to grace and glory through Their mediation. But the mode of the Incarnation and Divine Maternity becomes redemptive. Consequently, Scotus and the entire Franciscan school proclaim that, after the fall, all graces come to us through the Sacrifice of Jesus and Mary on Calvary (Mary's role being always secondary, subordinate to and dependent on that of Christ). The Passion of Christ and the Compassion of Mary are at the center of any authentic Christian spirituality, but especially any authentic Franciscan spirituality.

Contrasting consequences of the thomistic thesis

It is worth noting that the thomists uphold the doctrine of the mediation of Christ and His Mother through redemption; however, their position draws markedly different conclusions about the *reason* for Christ's mediation. They hold that the sole reason for the Incarnation is redemption from sin. In subordinating the Incarnation to Adam's fall, they necessarily subordinate the whole of Christ's mediation to sin. If one accepts this position, then all of the blessings of the Incarnation would be occasioned by sin.

Allow me to spell this out…participating in the divine nature through the mediation of Jesus Christ would be occasioned by sin; being coheirs with Christ, occasioned by sin; being adopted children of God in Christ Jesus, occasioned by sin; the revelation of the Trinity through Jesus and the unveiling that God is love through the Incarnation, occasioned by sin. The consequence of the thomistic thesis is that Jesus Christ, the Alpha and Omega, the pinnacle of all creation, the greatest work of God *ad extra*, is Himself occasioned by sin and we should rejoice in Adam's fall—in fact, the humanity of Christ should rejoice in Adam's fall—because without original sin there would not have been an Incarnation at all.

Taken a step further, this position subordinates the privileges, the mediation, and some would say even the existence of the Blessed Virgin Mary to Adam's fall[83]— no sin would mean no Mother of God, no maternal Mediatrix of graces, no spiritual Mother, no Queen of the angels and saints.

Scotistic Mariology, on the other hand, refuses to subordinate Mary's maternal mediation to sin.[84] Thus in Mariology maternal mediation has the primacy and coredemption is subordinate to it; although it must be noted that coredemption is a supreme manifestation of

---

83 See footnotes 11 and 12 in this study.

84 Cf. Fr. Ruggero Rosini, OFM, *Mariologia del beato Giovanni Duns Scoto*, c. III, art. I; he dedicates 4 pages to coredemption within the 50 page section on Mary's mediation. Nonetheless, in terms of the doctrinal premises establishing the very possibility of Marian coredemption the contribution of Scotus to the theology of coredemption is a major and decisive one.

Mother Mary's mediation. What makes this possible, and indeed the very concept of Marian coredemption plausible in the light of the matchless dignity of the Redeemer, is precisely Scotus' principles and the Franciscan thesis on the absolute, joint predestination of Jesus and Mary, a mystery making possible our cooperation in the work of redemption via the unique cooperation of Mary as Mother of God. St. Maximilian writes:

> Mary, by the fact of being the Mother of Jesus Savior, *became* the Coredemptrix of the human race, while, by the fact that She *is* the Spouse of the Holy Spirit, takes part in the distribution of all graces.[85]

With and subordinate to Christ the one Mediator, the Immaculate is absolutely predestined as Mediatrix of all graces. Her predestination and her role of Mediatrix is not relative to sin; rather, because of sin Christ the Mediator takes on the role of Redeemer and the Immaculate the role of Coredemptrix. And for Their *fiat* to the work of redeeming mercy: that of Mary at the Annunciation (cf. Lk. 1:38) matching that of Christ coming into the world at the same moment (cf. Heb. 10:5-10), we are forever grateful.

Ave Maria!

---

[85] St. Maximilian Kolbe, *Scritti*, 1229 (the italics were added); cf. 1224.

Conclusion

At the heart of theology is the mystery of charity: within the Trinity, and then in the economy of salvation. *"God is love"* (1 Jn. 4:8), God who is Father, Son and Holy Spirit. Consequently, all of His decrees are decrees of love and all of His actions are acts of love. The Most Holy Trinity, who is an eternal, loving communion of three Divine Persons in one Divine Essence, freely willed to communicate His love to a created nature outside Himself. He willed to do this in the most perfect way possible, namely by the union of the created, human nature of Christ with the divine nature in the Person of Word.

Jesus Christ, the Word made flesh, is therefore the first one predestined to grace and glory in the mind of God. Here is His Masterpiece! Here is the Incarnate Word who is most perfectly glorified and exalted by the Most Holy Trinity as King of all creation! Here is the Lord Jesus who most perfectly glorifies, adores and loves the Triune Godhead!

Christ, then, because He is predestined to grace and glory for His own sake, is not "occasioned" by anything. Rather, if anything exists outside of God it exists precisely for Christ. All things fall under His headship as the sovereign King of the universe. And our King has an absolute primacy which is not contingent upon man's need for redemption.

In the divine intention God chose that the Eternal Word assume His human nature by being *"born of a woman"* (Gal. 4:4). As a result, the Blessed Virgin Mary is predestined as the Mother of the Incarnate Word in the same decree that predestines Christ. She too is predestined absolutely as the universal Queen and Mother; she too has primacy over all creation—a subordinate primacy inseparable from that of Christ.

This means that God, before creating the universe, first foresees Christ the King and His Mother, the Queen. *"Before the foundation of the world"* (Eph. 1:4) God predestines Them. He foreordains that They be perfectly glorified by His divine love and foresees that They will respond perfectly to that love. This reality is symbolized by the fire blazing forth from the Sacred Heart of Jesus and the Immaculate Heart of Mary—two Hearts burning with love for the one true God.

God further wills to create angels and men that they might be *"holy and without blemish in His sight"* (Eph. 1:4). This is accomplished in and through Jesus and Mary, *"to the praise of His glory"* (Eph. 1:12). Thus He predestines the angels and elect to grace and glory in Christ. Jesus Christ and His Immaculate Mother are at the center of the divine plan from all eternity. They are the Mediator and Mediatrix of grace and glory to angels and men. Indeed all creatures exist for the Sacred Hearts of Jesus and Mary and find blessings therein.

Jesus and His Immaculate Mother are, therefore, the manifestation of God's love towards His creatures. *"In this has the love of God been shown in our case, that God has sent His only-begotten Son into the world that we may live through Him"* (1 Jn. 4:9). The Incarnation is first and foremost a manifestation of God's elevating love. God predestines us to be His adopted children in Christ, the Son of Mary; God divinizes us, that is, makes us sharers in His divine life through Jesus and Mary. With the Sacred Hearts placed by divine decree at the center of God's creative plan from all eternity, we are filled with wonder and gratitude at the loving designs of our Creator.

While this plan is fixed and remains substantially the same independently of any consideration of sin, the fact is that Adam and Eve—created to prefigure Christ and Mary and to be blessed in Them—disobeyed God's law and fell. God, foreseeing Adam's fall, willed also the remedy to our sin: redemption.

Here is where all the thomists and scotists unite: on blood-stained Calvary. After the fall, all graces—both the elevating grace of deification and the redeeming grace of reconciliation with God—flow from the Pierced Hearts of the Redeemer and Coredemptrix. And this Redeemer renews His sacrifice of love at every Holy Mass in an unbloody manner! Jesus Christ crucified and risen, with

His Divine Mother at His side, is at the center of the universe and of our lives in the Most Blessed Sacrament of the Altar! Let us adore Jesus in the Holy Eucharist with all the angels and saints who adore Him in the everlasting Beatific Vision.

And I beheld, and I heard a voice of many angels round about the throne, and the living creatures and the elders, and the number of them was thousand of thousands, saying with a loud voice, 'Worthy is the Lamb who was slain to receive power and divinity and wisdom and strength and honor and glory and blessing.' And every creature that is in heaven and on the earth and under the earth, and such as are on the sea, and all that are in them, I heard them all saying, 'To Him who sits upon the throne, and to the Lamb, blessing and honor and glory and dominion, forever and ever.' And the four living creatures said, 'Amen,' and the elders fell down and worshipped Him who lives forever and ever (Apoc. 5:11-14).

Ave Maria!

Appendix

Latin texts of Bl. John Duns Scotus on the absolute primacy of Christ

✝ Ordinatio, III, d. 7, q. 3; ed. C. Baliç, Joannis Duns Scoti, doctoris mariani, theologiae marianae elementa...ad fidem codd. mss. (Sibenici, 1933) 4-7

"Sed hic sunt duo dubia: Primum, utrum ista praedestinatio praeexigat necessario lapsum naturae humanae, quod videntur sonare multae auctoritates, quae sonant Filium Dei numquam fuisse incarnatum si homo non cecidisset.

"Sine praejudicio potest dici quod, cum praedestinatio cujuscumque ad gloriam praecedat ex parte objecti naturaliter praescientiam peccati vel damnationis cujuscumque, secundum opinionem ultimam dictam dist. 41 primi libri, multo magis est hoc verum de praedestinatione illius animae quae praedestinabatur ad summam gloriam; universaliter enim ordinate volens prius videtur velle hoc quod est fini propinquius, et ita sicut prius vult gloriam alicui quam gratiam, ita etiam inter praedestinatos, quibus vult gloriam, ordinate prius videtur velle gloriam illi, quem vult esse proximum fini, et ita huic animae prius vult gloriam quam alicui alteri animae vult gloriam, et prius cuilibet alteri gloriam et gratiam quam praevideat illi opposita istorum habituum.

"...Sed nec fuisse redemptio, nisi homo pecasset, facienda; sed non propter illam solam videtur Deus praedestinasse illam animam ad tantam gloriam, cum illa redemptio sive gloria animae redimendae non sit tantum bonum, quantum est illa gloria animae Christi; nec est verisimile tam summum bonum in entibus esse tantum occasionatum propter minus bonum solum, nec es verisimile ipsum prius praeordinasse Adam ad tantum bonum quam Christum, quod tamen sequeretur. Immo et absurdius ulterius sequeretur, scilicet quod praedestinando Adam ad gloriam, prius praevidisset ipsum casurum in peccatum quam praedestinasset Christum ad gloriam, si praedestinatio illius animae tantum esset pro redemptione aliorum.

"Potest igitur dici quod prius natura quam aliquid praevidebatur circa peccatorem sive de peccato sive de poena, Deus praeelegit ad illam curiam caelestem omnes quod voluit habere angelos et homines, in certis et determinatis gradibus, et nullus est praedestinatus tantum, quia alius praevisus est casurus, ut ita nullum oporteat gaudere de lapsu alterius" (The reference to dist. 41 of the First Book of Sentences will be found in Scotus' *Opera omnia*, Vatican edition (1963) VI, 332ff.)

✤ *Ordinatio,* III (suppl.) d. 19; cod. Assisi com. 137, fol. 161v; ed. Vivès (Parisiis, 1894) XIV, 714

"Quantum ad primum, dico quod Incarnatio Christi non fuit occasionaliter praevisa, sed sicut finis immediate videbatur a Deo ab aeterno…tunc iste fuit ordo in praevisione divina: *primo* enim Deus intellexit se sub ratione summi boni; in *secundo* signo intellexit omnes alias creaturas; in *tertio* praedestinavit ad gloriam et gratiam, et circa alios habuit actum negativum, non praedestinando; in *quarto* praevidit illos casuros in Adam; in *quinto* praeordinavit sive praevidit de remedio quomodo redimerentur per passionem Filii, ita quod Christus in carne, sicut et omnes electi, prius praevidebatur et praedestinabatur ad gratiam et gloriam, quam praevideretur passio Christi, ut medicina contra lapsum, sicut medicus prius vult sanitatem hominis, quam ordinet de medicina ad sanandum." We have given the Latin as reproduced in the Vivès edition.

✤ *Opus Parisiense*, Lib. III, d. 7, q. 4; ed. Balič, 13-15

"…dicitur quod lapsus hominis est ratio necessaria hujus praedestinationis. Ex hoc quod Deus vidit hominem casurum, vidit eum per hanc viam redempturum, et ideo praevidit naturam humanam assumendam et tanta gloria glorificandam.

"Dico tamen quod lapsus non fuit causa praedestinationis Christi. Immo etsi nec homo nec angelus fuisset lapsus, nec plures homines creandi quam solus Christus, adhuc fuisset Christus praedestinatus sic. Istud probo: quia omnis ordinate volens primo vult finem, deinde immediatus illa quae sunt fini immediatiora; sed Deus est ordinatissime volens: ergo sic vult. Primo ergo vult se; et post se immediate, quantum ad extrinseca, est anima Christi; ergo primum post velle intrinseca, voluit gloriam istam Christo; ergo ante quodcumque meritum at ante quodcumque demeritum praevidit Christum sibi esse uniendum in unitate suppositi.

"Item, ut declaratum est in primo libro, in materia de praedestinatione, prius est praeordinatio et praedestinatio completa circa electos quam aliquid fiat circa reprobos *in actu secundo*, ne aliquis gaudeat ex perditione alterius quod sibi sit lucrum: ergo ante lapsum praevisum et ante omne demeritum, fuit totus processus praevisus circa Christum.

"Item, si lapsus esset ratio praedestinationis Christi, sequeretur quod summum opus Dei esset maxime occasionatum, quia gloria omnium non est tanta intensive quam fuit Christi, et quod tantum opus dimisisset Deus per bonum factum Adae, puta si non pecasset, videtur valde irrationabile.

"Dico ergo sic: Primo Deus diligit se, secundo diligit se aliis, et iste est amor castus; tertio vult se diligi ab illo qui potest eum summe diligere, loquendo de amore alicujus extrinseci; et quarto praevidit unionem illius naturae quae debet eum summe diligere etsi nullus cecidisset.

"Quomodo ergo sunt intelligendae auctoritates sanctorum ponentium quod Deus non fuisset mediator, nisi aliquis fuisset peccator, et multae aliae auctoritates quae videntur sonare in contrarium? Dico quod gloria est ordinata animae Christi et carni, sicut potest carni competere, et sicut fuit collata animae in assumptione; ideo statim fuisset collata carni, nisi quod propter majus bonum fuit istud dilatum, ut per mediatorem, qui potuit et debuit, redimeretur gens a potestate diaboli, quia majus bonum fuit gloria beatorum redimendorum per passionem carnis, quam gloria carnis Christi; et ideo in quinto instanti vidit Deus mediatorem venientem passurum, redempturum populum suum; et non venisset ut mediator, ut passurus et redempturus, nisi aliquis prius pecasset, neque fuisset gloria carnis dilata, nisi fuissent redimendi, sed statim fuisset totus Christus glorificatus."

✝ *Lectura Completa*, III, d. 7, q. 3; ed. Balič, 188

"Ad primum dubium videtur mihi dicendum...si minimus electus non fuit praedestinatus propter lapsum ac reparationem alicujus, multo fortius nec praedestinatio Christi, qui est caput electorum, habuit causam occasionariam, ut lapsum generis humani; immo, si genus humanum non fuisset ita lapsum, adhuc fuisset praedestinatus et natura unita Verbo."

✝ *Reportatio Barcinonensis,* II, d. 7, q. 3; ed. Balič, 183-184

"Unde, cum actus voluntatis divinae circa praedestinatos positivus in communi praecedat omnes actus voluntatis ejus vel circa reprobos vel circa lapsum quorumcumque, non videtur (quod) praedestinatio Christi, qui praedestinatus est esse caput caelestis curiae, fuerit occasionata ex lapsu vel demerito reproborum. Deus ergo primo amat seipsum, et huic propinquius est amare animam Christi habere summam gloriam in Verbo; et hoc fuit primo volitum inter omnia creata volita, et post subsistentia in Verbo fuit secundo volitum, quae fuit praevisa ante omne meritum, et per consequens ante omne demeritum."

Index of Scripture References

Index of Saints & Theologians

The Academy of the Immaculate Books

Obviously there is a need for good, solid devotional books on Marian Shrines and Saints outstanding in their love for the Blessed Mother and the Eucharistic Jesus. The Franciscans of the Immaculate are attempting to meet this need and flood the market with readable inspirational books at a reasonable cost.

All Generations Shall Call Me Blessed *by Fr. Stefano Manelli, FI* A scholarly, easy to read book tracing Mary's role in the Old Testament through prophecies, figures, and symbols to Mary's presence in the New Testament. A concise exposition which shows clearly Mary's place in the economy of Salvation.

Totus Tuus *by Msgr. Arthur Burton Calkins* provides a thorough examination of the Holy Father's thoughts on total consecration or entrustment to Our Lady based on the historic, theological and scriptural evidence. Vital in clearing away some misunderstandings about entrustment and consecration.

Jesus Our Eucharistic Love *by Fr. Stefano Manelli, FI* A treasure of Eucharistic devotional writings and examples from the Saints showing their stirring Eucharistic love and devotion. A valuable aid for reading meditatively before the Blessed Sacrament.

Virgo Facta Ecclesia *by Franciscan Friars of the Immaculate* is made up of two parts: the first a biography on St. Francis of Assisi and the second part on the Marian character of the Franciscan Order based on its long Marian tradition, from St. Francis to St. Maximilian Kolbe.

Padre Pio of Pietrelcina *by Fr. Stefano Manelli, FI* This 144 page popular life of Padre Pio is packed with details about his life, spirituality, and charisms, by one who knew the Padre intimately. The author turned to Padre Pio for guidance in establishing a new Community, the Franciscans of the Immaculate.

For the Life of the World *by Jerzy Domanski, OFM Conv.* The former international director of the Knights of the Immaculata and Guardian of the City of the Immaculate in Poland examines Fr. Kolbe's Eucharistic, spiritual life as a priest and adorer of the Eucharist, all in the context of his love of the Immaculate.

Come Follow Me *by Fr. Stefano Manelli, FI* A book directed to any young person contemplating a Religious vocation. Informative, with many inspiring illustrations and words from the lives and writings of the Saints on the challenging vocation of total dedication in the following of Christ and His Immaculate Mother through the three vows of religion.

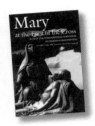

Mary at the Foot of the Cross I Acts of the International Symposium on Mary, Coredemptress, Mediatrix and Advocate. This over 400 page book on a week-long symposium held in 2000 at Ratcliffe College in England, has a whole array of outstanding Mariologists from many parts of the world. To name a few: Bishop Paul Hnilica, Fr. Bertrand De Margerie, S.J., Dr. Mark Miravalle, Fr. Stefano Manelli, FI, Fr. Aidan Nichols, O. P. , Msgr. Arthur Calkins, and Fr. Peter Fehlner, FI who was the moderator. Ask about books on similar symposiums in 2001-2005.

Not Made by Hands *by Thomas Sennott* An excellent resource book covering the two most controversial images in existence: the Holy Image of Our Lady of Guadalupe on the tilma of Juan Diego and the Sacred Image of the Crucified on the Shroud of Turin, giving scientific evidence for their authenticity and exposing the fraudulent carbon 14 test.

Devotion to Our Lady *by Fr. Stefano M. Manelli, FI* This book is a must for all those who desire to know the beauty and value of Marian devotion and want to increase their fervent love towards their heavenly Mother. Since it draws abundantly from the examples and writings of the Saints, it offers the devotee a very concrete and practical aid for living out a truly Marian life.

Do You Know Our Lady *by Rev. Mother Francesca Perillo, FI* This handy treatise (125 pages) covers the many rich references to Mary, as prefigured in the Old Testament women and prophecies and as found in the New Testament from the Annunciation to Pentecost. Mary's role is seen ever beside her Divine Son, and the author shows how scripture supports Mary's role as Mediatrix of all Graces. Though it can be read with profit by scripture scholars, it is an easy read for everyone. Every Marian devotee should have a copy for quick reference.

Who is Mary? *by Fr. Gabriele M. Pellettieri, FI* This book is a concise Marian catechism presented in a question/answer format. In this little work of love and scholarship the sweet mystery of Mary is unveiled in all its beauty and simplicity. It is a very helpful resource both for those who want to know the truth about Mary and those who want to instruct others.

A Month with Mary Daily Meditations for a Profound reform of the heart in the School of Mary *by Don Dolindo Ruotolo* This little book was written by a holy Italian priest Father Dolondo Ruotolo (1882-1970). Originallly written as spiritual thoughts to his spiritual daughter, the work is comprised of thirty-one meditations for the month of May. The month of Mary is the month of *a profound reform of heart:* we must leave ourselves and adorn ourselves with every virtue and every spiritual good.

Saints And Marian Shrine Series
Edited by Bro. Francis Mary, FI

A Handbook on Guadalupe This well researched book on Guadalupe contains 40 topical chapters by leading experts on Guadalupe with new insights and the latest scientific findings. A number of chapters deal with Our Lady's role as the patroness of the pro-life movement. Well illustrated.

St. Thérèse: Doctor of the Little Way
A compendium of 32 chapters covering many unique facets about the latest Doctor of the Church by 23 authors including Fr. John Hardon, SJ, Msgr. Vernon Johnson, Sister Marie of the Trinity, OCD, Stephanè Piat. This different approach to St. Thérèse is well illustrated.

Marian Shrines of France The four major Marian shrines and apparitions of France during the 19th century: Our Lady at Rue du Bac, Paris (Miraculous Medal), La Salette, Lourdes and Pontmain shows how in the 19th century — Our Lady was checkmating our secular, Godless 20th century, introducing the present Age of Mary. Well illustrated with many color pictures.

Padre Pio - The Wonder Worker The latest
on this popular saint of our times including the two
inspirational homilies given by Pope John Paul II during
the beatification celebration in Rome. The first part of the
book is a short biography. The second is on his spirituality,
charisms, apostolate of the confessional, and his great
works of charity.

Marian Shrines of Italy Another in the series of
"Marian Saints and Shrines," with 36 pages of
colorful illustrations on over thirty of the 1500
Marian shrines in Italy. The book covers that topic
with an underlying theme of the intimate and vital
relationship between Mary and the Church. This
is especially apparent in Catholic Italy, where the
center of the Catholic Faith is found.

Kolbe - Saint of the Immaculata Of all the
books in the Marian Saints and Shrines series, this one is
the most controversial and thus the most needed in order
to do justice to the Saint, whom Pope John Paul II spoke
of as "the Saint of our difficult century [twentieth]." Is it
true, as reported in a PBS documentary, that the Saint was
anti-Semitic? What is the reason behind misrepresenting

this great modern day Saint? Is a famous Mariologist right in accusing
the Saint of being in error by holding that Mary is the Mediatrix of
all Graces? The book has over 35 chapters by over ten authors, giving
an in-depth view of one of the greatest Marian Saints of all times.

The Academy of the Immaculate

The Academy of the Immaculate, founded in 1993, is inspired by and based on a project of St. Maximilian M. Kolbe (never realized by the Saint because of his death by martyrdom at the age of 47, August 14, 1941). Among its goals the Academy seeks to promote at every level the study of the Mystery of the Immaculate Conception and the universal maternal mediation of the Virgin Mother of God, and to sponsor publication and dissemination of the fruits of this research in every way possible.

The Academy of the Immaculate is a non-profit religious-charitable organization of the Roman Catholic Church, incorporated under the laws of the Commonwealth of Massachusetts, with its central office at Our Lady's Chapel, POB 3003, New Bedford, MA 02741-3003.

Special rates are available with 25% to 50% discount depending on the number of books, plus postage. For ordering books and further information on rates to book stores, schools and parishes: Academy of the Immaculate, 164 Charleston Ridge Dr., Mocksville, NC 27028, Phone/FAX (336) 751-2990, E-mail Mimike@pipeline.com. Quotations on bulk rates shipped directly by the box from the printery, contact: Franciscans of the Immaculate, P.O. Box 3003, New Bedford, MA 02741, (508) 996-8274, FAX (508) 996-8296, E-mail: ffi@marymediatrix.com., Web site, www. marymediatrix.com.